NEXT ERA
SELLING

5 Strategies to Make Your
Business Unstoppable

Anneke Seley   Britton Manasco

First Printing: 2016

ISBN: 978-0-9975900-0-5

www.nexteraselling.com

Ordering Information:
Special discounts are available on quantity purchases by corporations,
associations, educators and others.

For details, contact the publisher at 512-415-7936.

Dear friends and colleagues,

We're thrilled to share this executive briefing book with you.

In our consulting businesses, we have met hundreds of passionate executives, sales and marketing leaders, and growth-focused professionals who are challenging conventional practices. They are demonstrating that the selling and customer engagement strategies presented in this book produce superior results for shareholders, employees and buyers alike.

As someone seeking to understand the next era in selling, you know how exciting it is to build a revenue growth engine today. Inspired by folks such as you, we wrote this book — and have embarked on the next one — to share what we are discovering and learning.

Our collaboration started many years after we met at an Executive Summit of the AA-ISP (American Association of Inside Sales Professionals), where we found ourselves kicking around ideas late into the night. We've enjoyed exploring some big global themes together: the decline of distance, the rise of the remote, surmounting the *trust barrier*, making the virtual personal.

Our distinct, yet complementary, backgrounds — Britton's in marketing, messaging, and sales enablement; Anneke's in sales–model transformation, sales effectiveness, inside sales design and management — allowed us to look at emerging trends with new perspectives.

Thanks for your interest in our work and helping us share these ideas.

Anneke Seley and Britton Manasco

Contents

Introduction: Confronting the Virtual Selling Imperative   **1**

Strategy #1: Front Office Fusion   **5**

Unifying Your Front Office Teams   6

Front Office Fragmentation   7

Drivers of Change   8

What Needs to be Fused?   12

Fusing Digital and Human Interaction   14

Three Ways to Unify Your Front Office   15

Seizing the Power of Synergy   17

Strategy #2: The Inside Upside   **19**

What's Behind the Inside Sales Explosion?   20

Shackled to the Status Quo   21

Walls and Ceilings   22

Who Will Get Left Behind?   24

The Impact of Inside Sales   25

How Inside Sales Addresses a Weakness in Outside Sales   28

Repeatable, Predictable, Scalable   29

What to Expect as Inside Sales Expands   30

Strategy #3: The Outside Upside   **32**

What Separates the Outside from the Inside?   32

Mounting Pressures on Field Sales Organizations   33

Conventional Sales Structures in the Crosshairs   35

Building a Talent Pipeline   37

Focusing on the Strategic Few   39

Getting on the Grid   41

Tending the Toolset   43

Virtual, Yet Personal   44

Strategy #4: The Inside–Outside Alliance   46

Trending Now: Sales Development   46
Taking a New Direction   47
Standing Still: Implications and Consequences   48
Strategic Results through Collaboration   50
Pursuing Opportunities as a Team   50
The SDR Workflow   52
Measuring and Tracking Sales Development   53
Expanding through a Teaming Model   54
Who's the Quarterback?   56
Capitalizing on the Inside-Outside Alliance   57
Forward Together   59

Strategy #5: Networked Specialization   60

Unmet Needs, Increasing Expectations   60
What's Wrong with the Present State?   61
Specialization Deepens as Virtual Selling Increases   63
Want Executive Access? Enter the Statusphere   65
What's the Solution? How do You Get Access?   66
Addressing Complex and Technical Buyer Concerns   68
Unburdening Your Sales Reps   69
Collaborating as Complexity Intensifies   71
Specialize without Sacrifice   74

Conclusion: Rebalancing Your Sales Investment Portfolio   75

Acknowledgements   77

Endnotes   78

About the Authors   79

Introduction:

Confronting the *Virtual Selling Imperative*

Money is on the move. Large, established enterprises — the ones we refer to as "incumbents" — are seeking ways of going down market and expanding their sales coverage areas. Younger firms focused on high-growth — the ones we call "insurgents" — are looking to go up market. They want bigger, more strategic accounts, though they are wary of the expenses associated with traditional sales structures.

Whether your firm is an incumbent, insurgent or somewhere in between, there's likely a growing sense that the status quo is unsafe and unsustainable. After all, this is the era of perpetual "disruption." Even the disrupters — the innovators who've changed the game in their respective markets — are vulnerable to disruption over time. That is to be expected as we experience "the acceleration of everything."

But what do these dynamics mean for sales strategists?

What's clear is that business and sales leaders in all industries are intent on raising the returns on their sales investments. They're actively scrutinizing sales revenue to sales expense ratios, and too often, they don't like what they see. Even when sales expenses have been contained, there's a recognition that the sophistication of their selling organizations — and revenue generation teams overall — must rise to new levels.

This helps explain why business and sales leaders are now confronting something we call the *Virtual Selling Imperative*. It's a shift in selling strategy and practice that requires a rethinking of mindset, skillset and toolset. It's about transcending geography and other boundaries to break through the *Trust Barrier* with your buyers. It's about making the virtual truly personal.

Whether remote, digital, social or some mix, virtual selling is an increasingly prevalent way of engaging prospects and customers. And it's not confined to an inside sales organization. In fact, virtual selling is now infused into the work of high-performing inside, outside, account and channel-partner sales teams. But practicing it in an exceptional way demands new thinking and new designs.

So what explains this rise of the remote and decline of distance? What are the drivers of change? What's behind this *Virtual Selling Imperative*?

Here are three driving forces that make virtual selling increasingly attractive and pervasive:

1. Buyers want it. When stakes are high and deals are strategic, there are often many participants on a decision team. Bringing them all together for a face-to-face meeting can be extremely difficult, particularly if they are distributed geographically. When stakes are lower and deals are more transactional, there is often little perceived value in a face-to-face meeting. Buyers simply find it more convenient and less taxing to conduct business in virtual space. They have become progressively more comfortable with doing business at a distance. While deal sizes, support needs and other factors may create demand for on-site attention in some cases, it's clear buyers must now weigh those factors against the costs of conventional meetings.

2. Sellers want it. Corporate leaders are taking a closer look at the overall cost of sales. With this in mind, they are seeking ways to reduce costs and increase sales efficiencies. This motivation often encourages them to shift activity from a field sales organization to an inside sales organization. But it isn't just about cutting costs. Companies are also seeking ways of increasing market coverage. They want to penetrate underserved markets; they also want to expand into existing accounts. Virtual and remote selling practices can facilitate these efforts. Finally, there's an opportunity to experiment in new and unproven markets. Sales initiatives that otherwise would prove cost-prohibitive become possible through virtual selling.

3. Advances in technology, process and professionalism support it. What's also apparent is ongoing advancements and improvements associated with selling, communication and collaboration technology. Every year, networks become more capacious, computing power more massive, and software more intelligent and supportive. Remote communication, as a result, becomes increasingly rich and vivid. We can exchange volumes of information and levels of insight through screen-to-screen interactions that we might struggle to convey in person. But it's not just technology that enables these powerful interactions. Companies have made enormous strides in terms of supporting and enabling their sales professionals, providing ongoing coaching and data-driven feedback. When salespeople spend a great deal of time plugged into a matrix of pulsing information flows, they tend to learn and progress at a far faster rate than salespeople who operate in greater isolation — perpetually disoriented and disrupted by travel.

With all these forces at work, the case for virtual selling becomes increasingly powerful.

That said, it's worth recognizing that no one is arguing explicitly, or on principle, against virtual or remote selling. Indeed, some sales leaders and professionals might suggest there's nothing new here. After all, most field salespeople already spend a great deal of time on the phone and engaged in various digital interactions.

Why shake things up or suggest a good shaking is needed?

At this point, it's important to recognize this is largely an argument of degree, commitment and investment. But differences of degree, as we see it, are now critical to success.

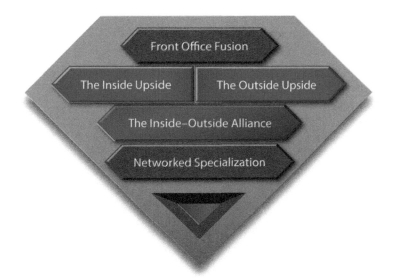

In this executive briefing book, we offer actionable strategies that are delivering clear and visible results. Among them:

Strategy #1: Front Office Fusion. By unifying and aligning the front office (sales, marketing, professional services and customer care/success), companies are spanning silos that might have otherwise led to bad handoffs and poor service. Instead, professionals in these various roles are actively collaborating to deliver an exceptional customer experience every time.

Strategy #2: The Inside Upside. By raising the ceilings and lowering the walls that have previously confined inside sales teams, firms have liberated them to expand their territories and coverage areas. They've raised quota sizes and average deal sizes, bringing new levels of respect, enthusiasm and opportunity to professionals in these roles.

Strategy #3: The Outside Upside. By encouraging field or outside reps to take on increasingly strategic deals and accounts, companies are enabling reps to become true consultants and trusted experts. They narrow their funnels, going deeper with fewer accounts while delegating transactional sales work to the inside sales team.

Strategy #4: The Inside–Outside Alliance. By facilitating and encouraging collaboration between inside and outside sales teams, firms are expanding their market coverage and coordination while bringing new levels of professionalism to their existing and prospective customers.

Strategy #5: Networked Specialization. As buyers seek more guidance and support in promising markets, firms are leveraging the expertise of specialists to address their needs. With an average of five team members associated with every buying decision, the rapid and parallel deployment of specialists — in a highly virtual and distributed environment — meets the needs of decision stakeholders. Trusted experts can open up executive doors that otherwise might remain closed and solve complex problems that would otherwise go unsolved.

In this emerging era of virtual selling, you can pursue strategies that previously would have been cost prohibitive. You can open up markets that would have proved elusive. You can run experiments that would have been too expensive or difficult to run. You can engage buyers in compelling new ways, bringing guidance that moves them to act — and leads them to success.

In *Next Era Selling*, we draw on the experiences of recognized firms, such as IBM, EMC, Oracle, ADP, SAP and Salesforce.com, as well as high flyers, such as Curvature, HubSpot, ServiceNow, ZipRecruiter, TriNet and Act-On Software, to illustrate our key themes and arguments.

To enter the vanguard of next era performers, you'll need to clarify how to invest your limited sales resources for maximum returns. You'll need to know why it matters to move from costly and conventional strategies to virtual selling strategies that make you unstoppable.

Strategy #1: Front Office Fusion

One of the central arguments made by "reengineering" experts back in the 1990s was that corporations had undermined their own performance by organizing around rigidly defined functional silos. That helped explain, for instance, the prior unraveling of Detroit automakers (and other American manufacturers) in the face of fierce Japanese competition.

By introducing processes that spanned these silos, the reengineers argued, companies could streamline operations and eliminate massive waste.

They could also enhance the customer experience in terms of product quality, response times and overall service levels. As management guru Michael Hammer wrote, "A company that does not focus resolutely on its customers and the processes that produce value for its customers is not long for this world."[1]

Well, fast forward to the present.

It seems the tendency toward functional silos and separation has reasserted itself in many established corporations. That is particularly true in the front office. It's a phenomenon that manifests itself in misalignment.

Marketing, sales and service organizations fragment into many disconnected specialties. As a result, huge investments in customer engagement and sales enablement produce little return. You have marketing people creating messages and materials salespeople in the field rarely use. According to the American Marketing Association, 90% of the materials marketing creates for selling teams do not get used.

Just as toxic and typical is the finger-pointing that occurs when pipelines dry up and quotas aren't met. You have demand-generation specialists complaining about the incompetence or laziness of sales. And you have salespeople complaining about the inadequacy or insufficiency of the leads they are given.

But even when functional specialists are not thwarting each other's interests, there's a growing need to unify and align the work of different groups. This challenge is particularly pronounced in the front office. Customers increasingly expect their experience with your company to be seamlessly managed across channels and touch-points. This is what gives them confidence in your solutions and emboldens them to invest.

This is a strategy we refer to as "Front Office Fusion." It's a critical element in efforts to address the *Virtual Selling Imperative*. And it will be a significant part of any well-balanced sales investment portfolio.

Unifying Your Front Office Teams

It's about unification. It's about bringing together departments, teams and professionals that might have otherwise been isolated in discrete silos.

Just as Michael Hammer laid out the argument that corporations have become specialized in a dysfunctional way, we are making the case that it's time to rethink how the participants in front office value creation work together.

You now need to focus on collaboration and boundary spanning, workflows and workstreams, process discipline and organizational (re)design. Only then can you fully develop and capitalize on the specialized talents of your people.

While smaller companies tend to struggle with an absence of specialization more than the excessive and dysfunctional specialization that hinders larger firms, it's clear that companies of all sizes need to be thinking strategically about how they unify their front office operations if they are to maximize their growth-oriented investments.

In this sense, sales organizations may need to seek opportunities to pool budget dollars and establish boundary-spanning initiatives if they are to yield maximum returns. Sales leaders may control their own investments, but likely don't control all investments that must be made to achieve Front Office Fusion. Nevertheless, they have enormous influence. They'll need the cooperation and shared commitment of marketing, service, product and, perhaps, other functional leaders to ensure silos are effectively spanned.

And fusion, like all other strategies discussed here, is multifaceted. Success in this endeavor is a matter of structure, talent, enablement and motivation. This may require shared compensation plans that encourage and reinforce collaboration. It certainly requires systems that facilitate the movement of information and provide a single view of the customer. But, to a great extent, customer-focused fusionism is a cultural and leadership commitment.

Leaders of the Austin-based inside sales team for Box.com have certainly recognized the power of fusion. With a fast-growing operation that encompasses marketing, sales development, account sales and customer success, managers focus on ensuring there is collaboration between individuals in different roles. This goal has influenced everything from sales coaching to seating arrangements within the firm's sales center. The team has even has even appointed a "demand czar," devoted to facilitating collaboration between marketing and sales specialists. This boundary spanner's objective is to ensure marketing campaigns are aligned with sales prospecting efforts, inbound leads are handed off effectively, and appropriate levels of follow-up are demonstrated.

Front Office Fragmentation

As with other strategies presented here, leaders will tend to look at them differently based on whether they consider their companies to be incumbents or insurgents.

The incumbent, or established, firm will tend to struggle with inflexible silos and excessive specialization. There's a tendency toward process breakdown. They may have much to unlearn or overcome. Existing incentives may impede collaboration.

Insurgents, on the other hand, may have very little to resist. They can design their organizations from the start in a unified fashion. However, they often struggle to specialize appropriately. Everyone is wearing a lot of hats in the front office. There's a tendency to take on more responsibility than one should, failing to delegate activities over time as progress demands.

Front Office (Con)Fusion

Source: Visible Impact and Reality Works Group

Either way, you'll struggle if you lack a truly fusionist front office design. Here are some of the patterns that manifest themselves:

- **Fragmentation and misalignment.** In this case, you have functional teams that don't collaborate effectively. You may have marketing and sales teams that can't agree on the definition of a lead, for instance, because no unifying process exists. Or you might have content or messages that were created in marketing silos, resulting in confusion when delivered by inside or field salespeople.

- **Breakdowns and ball-dropping.** Here, you may suffer from poor handoffs or no handoffs. You might have service and support people who have had customers abruptly "flipped" to them as salespeople move on to the next target. In this situation, the sales team might have no tangible stake in the customer's outcome. Yet another documented failure is slowness in responding to inbound leads, an issue that can dramatically reduce conversion rates. With every hour that passes, a prospect's receptiveness recedes.

- **Unmet needs and unaddressed concerns.** You may have prospective customers who are bewildered by a new product or fail to understand the value proposition. Why? Perhaps it is still presented in a needlessly complex way, because the product team didn't collaborate with marketing and sales on messaging. Maybe sales engineers were not brought into the selling process at the right time or in the right way to address concerns and questions.

When front offices are not unified, it's common for work product (messages, leads, opportunities, etc.) to be simply thrown "over the wall." That may end up leaving an impression with your customer that your various units or departments don't communicate.

As opposed to ensuring a smooth transition and effective collaboration, functional teams merely pursue narrow agendas and objectives. Such behavior, unsurprisingly, manifests itself in added costs, inflexible operations and a diminished customer experience. Sales teams, meanwhile, mightily struggle to meet quota and hit their goals, while customer success professionals face an increase in customer churn.

Drivers of Change

Despite all the division and disarray we see on the wider corporate landscape, it's clear change is happening, and companies are seeking greater unity in the front office. There's an intent and an opportunity to guide buyers through the full Customer Success Cycle, from awareness to advocacy.

Rising expectations associated with the customer experience represent the most significant driver of change. Buyers, obviously, have a wealth of options and offers to consider. They aren't interested in working with companies whose seams are always showing.

The Customer Success Cycle

Source: Visible Impact and Reality Works Group

It's also apparent more companies are organizing around account or customer management instead of products. Established firms can't afford to have divisional salespeople tripping over each other within an account and undermining the brand. Meanwhile, start-ups and expansion-stage firms are intent on ensuring the lifetime value and annual recurring revenue of their clients exceed customer acquisition cost. They are focusing on customer success as opposed to merely short-term measures of revenue.

Act-On Software, a leader in marketing automation solutions for small- and mid-size businesses, achieved three-year sales growth of 932% by applying these principles. Shawn Naggiar, who spent nearly seven years as the firm's chief revenue officer (and is now chief business officer at Moxtra), describes the creation of a "predictable machine" fueled by inbound marketing leads that were then managed by sales development and inside sales reps. "From an economics standpoint, it's a fully repeatable model," he says.

But success in cloud-based software demands attention to customer loyalty and avoidance of churn. Unlike enterprise software models of the past, recurring revenue models, such as Act-On's, demand close cooperation between reps and customer success managers. "In the past, it was rare for sales leaders to worry about customer service," Naggiar adds. "But this is changing. Smart organizations will increasingly merge sales and customer success."

To win in this environment, you have to unify as an organization. You have to successfully guide buyers through their journey and deliver an exceptional experience.

Designing the right departmental goals, objectives and incentives is the first step toward Front Office Fusion. We've worked with many a company that rewards one department for activities and results that don't help — or actively harm — another. This is an especially prevalent problem in sales and marketing. Here's a typical scenario:

Marketing is recognized, compensated and promoted based on the delivery of leads or appointments to sales. While demand generation, content marketing, social and e-mail marketing professionals are celebrating monthly or quarterly bonuses, their sales colleagues may be wasting time following up on the wrong prospective opportunities at the wrong time.

Front Office Fusion

Source: Visible Impact and Reality Works Group

Some companies are alleviating this problem by tying bonus compensation to specific sales metrics by setting targets for marketing's contribution to both forecast and revenue. The Pedowitz Group describes the concept of "Revenue Marketing" as the kind of marketing that consistently produces predictable and scalable sales results.

"This means that not only can marketing report on revenue attribution, it can also predict it," according to Pedowitz. "Just like a VP of sales takes a given revenue number and does backwards math to see what needs to go into the top of the funnel to get to that ultimate number, the VP of marketing takes a similar approach and comes to the table with a Revenue Marketing Forecast that aligns tightly with sales to ensure the revenue goal is reached. Marketing is a revenue center at this stage."[2]

Once these aligned marketing and selling goals, incentives and processes are in place, marketing teams must provide compelling content that attracts buyers, then hand them off to sales professionals when the time is right. Sales openers will build on the awareness and interest created by marketing, qualify prospects and set up appointments for closers. Sales closers, in turn, will gracefully hand new customers off to account managers (or customer success managers), who will nurture and grow them.

Sophistication about the interplay of these different roles and teams continues to grow every day. Thanks to the growing capabilities of today's "systems of engagement" (or customer relationship management systems), it is becoming easier to track customers over time and across organizational boundaries. You can ensure the right action is taken at the right time by the right professional. Front office teams collaborate to create customer value.

In turn, these systems of engagement — a term coined by pioneering management theorist Geoffrey Moore — change the nature of front office work: They make it more visible and open to redesign.

You can even redesign roles and unbundle aspects of them into micro-steps in a wider process. That's what happens, for instance, when you take lead research off the salesperson's back and hand it to a specialized researcher.

Or you can unify activities that once were separately handled. Marketing, for instance, can see when sales accepts a lead (based on jointly established criteria), track the lead forward to ensure it is acted on, then determine when (and if) it enters the forecast and is eventually closed (or lost). Sales, meanwhile, can see exactly how marketing is generating the leads that are being presented. Customer success teams, in turn, can track deal progression, anticipate when an opportunity will likely close and be ready with an onboarding plan. Visibility of this sort helps ensure execution and accountability.

Sometimes collaboration across boundaries even leads to increased deal sizes. "Our marketing team was clinging to preconceived notions about how people buy, because of what they saw when no salesperson was involved," says Kevin Gaither, vice president of sales at ZipRecruiter. "Once my inside sales team started calling older and abandoned leads, we started seeing higher average order values and a different way of closing business. This triggered marketing to take a fresh look at what could be achieved. The marketing team learned from inside sales how to present the product to our online purchasers to achieve higher average order values."

New business models, particularly in the technology sphere, are changing the game, too. As Harvard Business School's Michael Skok argues, companies now must create "addiction before adoption and expansion." In other words, they increasingly must give away valuable content or provide "freemium" versions of their products merely to attract customers. But this model breaks down, unless the organization is then able to effectively move customers into adoption and expansion stages. Tight linkages between groups are needed to guide customers through this life cycle.

Switching costs are lower than ever, reducing the customer's barriers to exit. As companies embrace business models based on customer engagement and limited lock-in, they can no longer afford mistakes that would have been acceptable in the past. Now, every group — product, marketing, sales and service — must ensure it is tightly aligned with others to provide an experience that attracts, grows and retains customers.

What Needs to be Fused?

It's useful to consider some of the different teams in the front office that need to be unified if companies are to perform at their optimum. While there are certainly others to be considered in the mix, here are some of the key business functions:

- **Product.** The product development and marketing teams have a critical role in the design of the customer experience. And that's just the point. The experience is the product. It's critical to consider the interactions a prospect will have with both the product and the provider. How is the solution's value comprehended, realized and shared? Beyond design and development, product experts can play an invaluable role in efforts to articulate and communicate value at all stages of a buyer's journey. They must collaborate with marketing and sales to do so. They must collaborate with account and success managers (and even professional service or implementation teams) to grasp the full impact of a product or solution offering when it has been sold.

- **Marketing.** In recent years, marketing has begun to play an increasingly active role in companies, particularly as its results have become more trackable and measurable. Once relegated to discrete activities such as branding, advertising and public relations, it now is expected to handle activities such as demand generation and sales support. Success depends on deep alignment with the sales organization to meet these objectives. Marketing and selling teams must come together around issues such as messaging, lead definition and pipeline development. Marketing often owns "voice of the customer" responsibility, as well. It collaborates with product teams to bring empathy and insight to the product design (and customer interaction) process. And marketing efforts to amplify the success stories of customer advocates — which depend on coordination with account managers — play a critical role in the attraction of new customers.

- **Sales.** Team selling is a watchword in many companies these days, a reflection of the growing number of intersecting roles and actions within sales itself. In many cases, field salespeople rely on inside salespeople (or sales/business development reps). They also require the active assistance of sales engineers, deal-desk professionals and other sales support personnel.

Another essential is the linkage of quota-carrying new-business sales reps (aka "hunters") and customer success, account or renewals reps (aka "farmers"). They have to collaborate to ensure the customer is successfully onboarded and engaged. And, as mentioned, sales teams increasingly collaborate with marketing teams in the development of messages, content, tools and customer demand. To ensure the right quality and quantity of leads are produced, sales must synchronize its efforts with marketing on everything from targeting to win/loss to churn analysis.

- **Customer Success/Account Management.** When companies seek to "land and expand," and retain customers, account reps play a critical role in the expansion phase. Whether they are the initiators or coordinators of new selling activity, account managers are the ongoing eyes and ears into accounts, assisted by customer usage data. The fact that some firms have begun to shift from a customer service/support orientation to "customer success" is also noteworthy. This reveals the growing recognition, particularly in arenas where recurring revenue is critical, that success depends on both customer enthusiasm and advocacy, not merely satisfaction or passive loyalty. But to be exceptional in these roles, account and success managers must effectively collaborate with reps who close deals and marketers who celebrate customer wins. Of course, the most important collaboration someone in this role must undertake is with the customer. That means being the face of the supplier organization in relation to all resources the client might value or require.

- **Partners and Other Third Parties.** Active collaboration need not simply be intra-firm. It can also be inter-firm. This is especially important for alliances companies have with their channel, service, technology and supply-chain partners. This is one place where virtual communication and collaboration become especially critical. To a great extent, you organize and orchestrate your ecosystem through virtual engagement. Your partners may rely on your experts to clarify value or close sales, solve technical problems, or address customer support issues. You are challenged to deploy your resources in an agile and efficient manner to cost-effectively maintain and strengthen these relationships. But other partners may also play a critical role in your front office endeavors. Whether it's an appointment setting or lead generation firm or sales training partner, these parties play an important role in your go-to-market efforts. You extend your value to clients by making your partners an extension of your organization.

Obviously, there's a wide array of potential connections and relationships involving the parties mentioned here. And there are other parties (including back office functions and specialists) that have not been mentioned. The array of possible permutations and interactions only grows as a company evolves and becomes more specialized. Whatever the layout of your front office, parties must unify and actively collaborate to create customer value in this increasingly demanding era.

Fusing Digital and Human Interaction

Apart from the functional perspective on fusionism, it's worth considering other ways in which a fusionist point of view is valuable.

One lens to consider is the fusion of human and digital interactions with customers. There's certainly been a great deal of attention placed in recent years on what activities can be automated and handled by machines. Take marketing automation, for instance. There's enormous enthusiasm around automating lead generation or even "demand creation." Some marketers even suggest that, ultimately, human interaction will be virtually irrelevant. Just let buyers guide themselves.

But the reality is, in many cases (and nearly all cases involving a complex or high-stakes sale), the best buyer outcomes revolve around the successful interplay of human and digital interaction. (And, of course, all digital interaction isn't necessarily automated; successful interactions via email or social media can depend on highly personal attention.) You win when you effectively deploy people who can empathize and interact in ways that are not easily handled (or possible at all) through digital automation.

In a recent study conducted by SiriusDecisions on B2B buyers, researchers Marisa Kopec and Jennifer Ross found that buyers interact with sales representatives at every stage of the buying cycle, and sales presentations were ranked as the "most impactful" events in terms of facilitating a decision. The B2B buying journey, they added, is "not linear."[3]

You may encourage your prospects to download position papers, watch videos, read reports, or visit blogs. But when do you pick up the phone and make a truly human connection? When do you make it personal and contextually relevant by diving deeper into the specific circumstances of that prospect's world? When the stakes are high (or relatively high), you can't anticipate all the prospect's concerns with pre-produced content. You may not even be able to convey warmth and authenticity, or even build the right level of trust with your prospect, unless you make a real, live connection that goes beyond digital formats.

Circumstances are shaped by the buyer's preferences and risk appetite. We know of half-million dollar deals that have been closed through email or a chat session. It happens — though it's worth looking at what might have happened previously to build the necessary foundations for trust. The bottom line? The fusion of both human and digital elements deserves careful attention in customer interaction design.

Three Ways to Unify Your Front Office

While the challenge of front office fragmentation is often tremendous, there are a number of key actions you can take to overcome this issue. When you embrace and invest in a Front Office Fusion strategy, though, you have to recognize you must span boundaries. You may even need to pool budget dollars with other functional organizations to get things done. Sales leaders, most assuredly, must collaborate with leaders in marketing, service and other areas. Sales ops teams must actively engage marketing ops teams, and so on.

If you're successful, you can close the *Guidance Gap* your prospective buyers need you to help them close. You can provide the insight and support they need — when they need it — to clarify the case for change and justify a buying decision.

Closing the Guidance Gap

Source: Visible Impact and Reality Works Group

But you have to determine where to start or, more precisely, where to make your most significant investments. You aren't likely to be starting from zero. Rather, you are likely making greater commitments to a cause that may have been previously (if vaguely) identified.

So here are three ways to execute a Front Office Fusion strategy:

Unify marketing and sales messaging. Whether you're a marketing professional focused on campaigns or a sales professional who gets results from conversations, much is riding on the message you convey. Your message will either attract and engage prospective buyers or it won't. But one thing's for sure: Multiple, discordant messages will only confuse and repel them. You have to unify your messaging across the organization — and make it relevant and compelling — if you are to engage buyers.

There are many reasons this doesn't happen. Too often, the message simply doesn't hit the mark. It isn't on point. It isn't provocative or interesting or relevant to your buyer. Insufficient effort may have gone into creating it. Perhaps it's all about you and your products. Perhaps it doesn't lock onto the searing pain points your prospects might be experiencing in the absence of your solution.

But even when interesting content is created, it's not at all clear that messages created and disseminated by marketing teams in their content marketing efforts will be reflected in sales interactions and conversations. In fact, there's plenty of evidence to suggest that misalignment is common in messaging. This undermines customer engagement.

To overcome this challenge, it's critical for experts in sales, marketing and product to come together around messaging-development efforts. By producing messaging based on consensus and commitment across boundaries, you ensure messages are delivered with conviction by salespeople. They bring insights, perspectives and a point of view based on the collective understanding of your front office brain trust. That's how you get from campaigns that attract and entice to conversations that clarify and motivate.

Unify demand creation. Remarkable strides have been made in recent years when it comes to lead and demand generation. Companies have made significant investments in efforts to establish processes, train teams and roll out technologies that enhance the lead generation and nurturing processes. These efforts have, in many cases, contributed mightily to sales pipeline volume and velocity.

But performance variances are everywhere, and commitment is uneven across the business landscape. Success stories associated with investments in marketing automation technology are proliferating. Yet there is still much to be done in terms of realizing the promise.

This is an opportunity for front office teams to come together. Some sales and marketing organizations, for instance, have relied on SiriusDecisions to create an entirely new vocabulary and introduce new practices. The firm's "Demand Waterfall" methodology has enabled groups to track the transference of a "Marketing Qualified Lead" (MQL) to sales as a "Sales Accepted Lead" (SAL).

By creating accepted definitions for leads at different stages of maturity, such methodologies have proved a powerful way to unite organizational functions that once had no objective means of managing lead flow and ensuring accountability. Reliance on marketing automation and customer relationship management technology, meanwhile, has provided increasing visibility to all parties and enables organizations to report on (and improve) performance. Expect more advances as these practices become more prevalent.

Unify your customer touch-points. Just as consumer-oriented enterprises have struggled with a proliferation of channels, business-oriented companies now must consider the opportunities and liabilities associated with their own channel choices. Buyers are now likely to experience your brand through an array of media and channels (web, email, social media, mobile apps, chat, phone, physical and virtual events, on-site/in person, etc.).

The question to consider is whether the buyer's experience is coherent, consistent and compelling, or somehow disjointed and disorienting. Much rides on ensuring sales interactions — be they in person or virtual — are consistent with marketing interactions that may have preceded them or service interactions that may follow.

Unifying these touch-point interactions is an essential challenge going forward, particularly as buyers increasingly expect a "consumer-grade" experience when engaged in B2B buying decisions. Not only must these interactions across media and touch-points be consistent, but consistently compelling.

This explains why companies are increasingly anxious to ensure the hand offs between functional organizations are seamless and streamlined. The buyer's journey is where companies may want to begin their customer-interaction design efforts. They can map out the journey from the customer's point of view, and work backward to organizational and touch-point design. While these concerns once might have been relegated to the B2C world, it's apparent B2B leaders are now taking them just as seriously.

Seizing the Power of Synergy

The term "synergy" was popularized by Buckminster Fuller, a pioneering architect and systems thinker. He warned against the dangers of excessive specialization. As he saw it: "Specialization has bred feelings of isolation, futility and confusion in individuals. It has also resulted in the individual's leaving responsibility for thinking and social action to others."[4]

Our view is there is a dynamic tension between synergy and specialization. You have to strike a balance, particularly as your organization grows. You should take Fuller's concerns to heart, but you shouldn't stop there. You have to recognize the power of both synergy and specialization, as you invest in your revenue-generating organization.

Front Office Fusion is a strategy that emphasizes unity, overlap and collaboration. In considering a strategic portfolio of sales investments, business leaders should look at how buyers experience their companies and ensure they are laying the foundations for unified work in the front office. It sets the stage for virtual selling by ensuring sales professionals have the insights, messages, tools, coaching and support they need to provide a personal and powerful experience at a distance. Fusionism makes it possible to draw on the strengths and skillsets of complementary specialists —when you need them. You can bring the full force and collective expertise of your organization to bear as you guide your buyers through demanding decisions.

One organization that is particularly elevated by fusionism is inside sales. As we explore in the next chapter and beyond, inside sales teams are emboldened by new technologies and new levels of professionalism. People in these roles are often learning at an accelerated rate. They are closing deals of increasing size and impact. But they are also empowered to capitalize on the work of marketing teams while demonstrating their value as facilitators of field sales success. That's the power of synergy.

Strategy #2: The Inside Upside

"I am surrounded by a bunch of people trying to figure out how to make inside sales acceptable or meaningful within their companies. They're clinging ... like a barnacle clinging to a rock. And this inferiority complex around the whole thing is bizarre. This is the engine of growth; it's not something to downplay or soft pedal."

That's how one frustrated executive described his experience at an exclusive meeting with other executive leaders in the inside sales profession. The implication is that inside sales has a self-confidence problem. It's an issue that's rooted in the past, yet alive and observable in the present culture of many companies — particularly larger, more established ones.

There's been a stigma associated with the "telemarketers in the cubicles" — or, at least, there's a stigma in the eyes of some sales leaders. Unfortunately, the leaders in the inside sales organization have, too often, bought into this mindset. Some compliantly act as the betas in a box, as the alpha dogs roam freely and hungrily in the field.

But something has been changing for quite a few years. The gravity of value creation in the selling profession is progressively and relentlessly shifting. Established enterprises in a growing number of industries are recognizing the true power of the inside sales organization — power that exceeds its reputation as a source of support for the field or even as a low-cost distribution channel.

Increasingly, inside sales is being seen as a driver of profitable growth — a force uniquely suited to new market exploration and, sometimes, deep account penetration.

Moreover, the inside sales organization is being recognized as a proving ground for future talent. It's a means of accelerating skill development and performance attainment. For some, it's a great place to start a career. For others, it's also a great place to work as one advances deep into a career. This pattern may prove to be even more consequential going into the future.

In fact, venture-backed start-ups now recognize inside sales as the core model for selling. Venture capitalists support it and even demand it. "This model is a competitive differentiator that will give companies a two-year lead in terms of their growth rate versus the old sales model," says Lars Leckie, a managing partner with Hummer Winblad. "Innovation isn't just for products; companies need innovation in sales, too."

Guess who else is starting to demand it. That's right: buyers.

They are embracing new options and offers that can only be made profitably through inside sales (or virtual selling) arrangements. The ongoing movement from high capital expenditures (capex) to offerings procured as operating expenses (opex) is further fueling this dramatic shift.

Buyers are simply becoming more comfortable with buying through virtual channels. Perhaps this pattern can be traced back to Amazon.com and pioneers in e-commerce. But it's clear buyers are increasingly contented making large purchases without face-to-face meetings.

Consequently, the case for you to make an active investment in inside sales has never been stronger.

What's Behind the Inside Sales Explosion?

Consider some of the indicators of growth and progress in today's inside sales movement.

Clearly, the inside sales profession is on a fast track. The field of inside sales is now growing at 5% annually in the United States, according to the Bureau of Labor Statistics and InsideSales.com. In fact, the number of inside sales reps rose to 2.5 million in 2015. That's three times faster than the growth of the field sales profession (which now has an estimated 8 million members).

U.S. Total Growth of Inside Sales

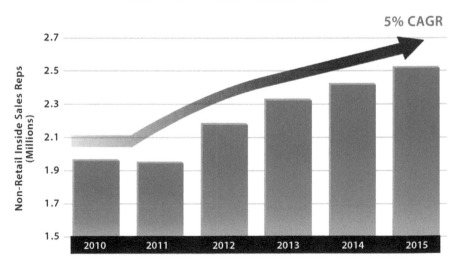

Source: U.S. Bureau of Labor Statistics, InsideSales.com

Research from the American Association of Inside Sales Professionals (AA-ISP) suggests that employers are now struggling to find enough people to fill inside sales roles. At the same time, the professionalism of inside sales is rising to new levels. Not only are professional training and certification programs available from organizations such as the AA-ISP, companies such as Oracle, SAP and Salesforce. com have built their own sales academies. Individuals in these roles are getting more training, coaching and personal development on the job than ever. They also are getting fast feedback and thoughtful performance reviews.

What's more, compensation levels are rising in the field as responsibility increases. New career opportunities are opening up. Young people, in particular, are finding opportunities to learn and develop their skill sets in ways that position them strongly for successful careers.

But it isn't just recent college grads who are benefiting from this pattern. It's benefiting professionals of all educational backgrounds, and all ages and ethnicities. Inside sales has become a training ground for a diverse and dynamic workforce. All that matters is that you perform.

Shackled to the Status Quo

Despite the impressive returns many companies are realizing through their inside sales investments, many others have resisted the trend. So what's holding them back? While some patterns play out across the board, resistance tends to be different in different types of organizations.

Established companies often struggle to capitalize on inside sales, which may suggest old school thinking is still dominant. "[M]any sales leaders have a personal bias toward deploying outside salespeople over inside sales," writes Steve W. Martin, a sales specialist associated with the USC Marshall School of Business. "In some cases, this inclination was based on their own experience from many years ago when they were in field sales."[5]

After all, senior sales executives in these companies have been successful pursuing certain game plans. They've met quotas and built their books of business through conventional field selling activities. If inside sales exists at all in these firms, it may merely play a minor or supporting role. The field salespeople are recognized as the real stars.

As a result, sales leaders may not even be familiar with the possibilities associated with inside sales as a growth engine. They intuitively resist any efforts to expand its dominion. And since former field salespeople often rise to top positions in sales organizations, they often don't respect inside sales directors and managers the way they do their field-based lieutenants.

Not surprisingly, resources, compensation structures and territorial arrangements play to the favor of the field organization. The inside sales group is confined and contained.

Just look at the structure of many established organizations. Inside sales managers report to leaders who either run the field or have a strong bias toward the field sales organization as the key revenue driver. It's how they've always operated. Why take risks on something new and unfamiliar? It could hurt the firm's stock price, or negatively affect commissions and bonuses. Those, anyway, are the types of concerns that impede change.

Unfortunately, inside sales weaknesses can be self-fulfilling prophecies. In the absence of respect, influence and investment, inside sales leaders are unable to build successful organizations or attract talented people. They are simply boxed in, shackled to the status quo.

Walls and Ceilings

There's a phenomenon in sales organizations we like to refer to as "walls and ceilings."

Start with the ceilings. While many inside sales organizations don't even have quota-carrying roles, quota carriers in other inside organizations experience concrete ceilings on compensation, deal size, and territorial reach.

Most companies seem to put hard and fast ceilings on deal sizes. In other words, when a deal reaches a certain size — say, $25,000 (or $100,000 in an established tech organization) — it will be taken away from the inside person and given to the field person.

Does this make sense? While sales forces need to be structured and segmented, existing ceilings often put convention and territoriality over talent and profit maximization. In many cases, these policies lead to deal sizes hovering just below the threshold, because no one has an incentive to push them over.

The walls are the barriers organizations put on human interaction with clients and prospects. They make assumptions about what types of communication are appropriate for an inside team. While they might let inside teams set appointments or handle high-volume outbound calling, they may not be allowed to give sales presentations or close deals. An occasional business trip or client meeting in the field — which some have referred to as being part of a "hybrid," inside/field sales role — may be out of the question; that kind of activity might be strictly reserved for a field sales team.

Such constraints, naturally, contribute to the perception of low status that often attends to inside sales. It puts severe constraints on career growth and trajectories.

Walls and Ceilings

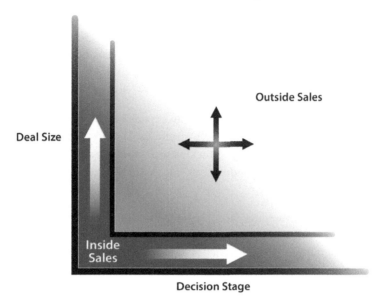

Source: Visible Impact and Reality Works Group

Of course, when inside sales roles are perceived as low status, teams are prone to perform as expected. No great gains will be made, and no breakthroughs will be witnessed. It's a huge missed opportunity — one that can harm both the seller and the buyer.

These are just some of the constraints imposed in large organizations. Consider the limitations that often hinder the growth of start-ups. While many young ventures are now actively embracing the inside sales model and are turning it into a powerful growth driver, others lack a sense of rigor, process and discipline with respect to the model.

Or maybe they aren't particularly interested in sales at all. In many venture-backed companies, the founders and executive leaders are technologists or engineers. They have no natural understanding of or attraction to the field of sales. If they could generate revenue some other way, they might abolish the function altogether.

This natural antipathy to the sales profession has created opportunities for marketing gurus to make questionable claims. These consultants suggest initiatives such as search engine marketing, social media marketing and content marketing make the sales organization practically irrelevant. They contend that buyers can buy on their own, and sellers should play a mere perfunctory role as "order takers" — assuming they are needed at all.

While certain business models may lend themselves to such strategies, this is a fanciful view for any company selling a high-value, high-impact solution. Even if your initial offers are low-cost (or even "freemium" in nature), it's eventually necessary to sell in a more skilled and personal way. Unless you're selling highly transactional products that buyers can fully evaluate and purchase on their own, you'll need consultative salespeople to grow accounts and expand once you've landed.

That isn't to suggest you will necessarily need an expensive field sales organization. Salesforce.com, for instance, initially grew on the back of an inside sales model. It was only later — when the company decided penetrating larger enterprises was critical to its growth — that investments in the field sales organization became more critical.

The bottom line is that young ventures can severely undermine their own growth potential and market valuations by pretending sales is an unnecessary expense and that buyers can simply buy on their own.

Who Will Get Left Behind?

So what are the implications and consequences of standing still?

Both incumbents and insurgents are at risk when they fail to properly invest in and recognize the full value of an inside sales organization. They will tend to have unmotivated and unenthusiastic employees operating in old-school contact centers. They will experience high turnover and long ramp times.

Established incumbents are particularly vulnerable to disappointing sales performance due to an overreliance on an expensive field organization. Worse, sometimes underperformance remains hidden due to faulty measures and assumptions. In fact, some sales organizations simply chase top-line revenue. In many cases, the profitability or lack thereof associated with field sales efforts is not fully recognized, assessed or examined.

Such companies become vulnerable to disruptors or rivals that bring different selling models to market and, as a result, can offer comparable products and services faster, more predictably and at reduced rates. They also become vulnerable to rivals that are simply more profitable at offering comparable offers. Why? Because their rivals are relying on inside sales channels that perform more profitably and with higher velocity.

Further, these incumbents are vulnerable to the changing demands and expectations of prospective customers. As buyers realize they can get faster answers and better deals without the typical hassles and frictions associated with field sales, they are prone to switch suppliers.

Finally, they are vulnerable to opportunity costs. Consider the untapped markets and underserved customers field-heavy sales forces cannot reach. They may be unable to target "micro-markets" because they lack the agility to do so. They are mired in physical geography at a time when location is of diminishing importance.

Without aggressive investments in inside sales, established companies are simply unable to seize new and emerging markets. They are unable to run trials and tests — exploring new messages, new offers and new target profiles to identify and surface new market opportunities. They are exposed to rivals who run faster and think smarter.

At the same time, startups and other insurgents run the risk of mishandling the Inside Upside if they improperly cultivate, support and coach their people. There are many challenges to address in the rollout and development of an effective inside sales organization. You need the right leaders, systems and procedures in place to consistently produce results.

Alternatively, insurgents may fail to grasp the markets available to them when they don't deploy actual humans in the sales process. They run the risk of being eclipsed by other fast movers with a more expansive view of market opportunities.

Recognize that people still buy from people when the stakes are high. While it's fine for buyers to buy certain items online and on their own, they want to know people are involved when they are making investments that have important implications and consequences. They want to know someone is considering the unique, personal, often idiosyncratic nature of their particular situations. It's just not clear you always have to meet with these people in person. In a growing number of situations, you don't.

The Impact of Inside Sales

Seizing the moment, companies of all sizes and in all industries are now aggressively investing in inside sales endeavors. There's clearly a spectrum in terms of how central these inside sales organizations are to their growth strategies. Nevertheless, money is on the move, and it's flowing in this direction.

Some established companies have made significant investments. Leading companies, such as Oracle, SAP, ADP and Thomson Reuters, have been quite vocal about their own investments and activities in the inside sales realm. IBM opened a new state-of-the-art digital sales center in Ireland in fall 2014 and in Cairo in early 2015.

As Judy Buchholz, general manager of IBM Digital Sales, explains: "Today's buyers land on our site and want to talk to someone through chat or video. These buyers are forcing a shift in the sales model to reps not bound by territory but rather defined by their ability to engage on a certain subject or topic."

"Inside sales is suited for the type of quick and convenient engagement today's service-oriented buyers expect," she adds. "It's a matter of equipping sellers to effectively use digital and social tools and techniques. Our reps can engage with prospects on chat or video, work with them to download the software or start a small cloud pilot, and then stay with them to see how they use the software."

Research from USC's Martin suggests companies in high technology and business services have been particularly quick to adopt the inside sales strategy. Asked to rank the most influential factors behind their investments, they pointed to:

- Increasing pressure on business performance and profitability (60%)

- Technology advancements (54%)

- Buyers who more readily accept the remote selling process (47%)

Interestingly, 84% of respondents stated that inside sales models allow them to onboard new salespeople and share best practices more easily, while 79% said the model would enable their sales organizations to scale faster.

"Today, there is a changing perception among sales leaders about the strategic role inside sales performs," Martin contends. "This change is due to the benefits that sales leaders believe the inside model provides, in terms of scaling activity, growing the organization and attacking specific markets."

The pattern that seems increasingly visible is a shift toward greater opportunity, autonomy and territorial reach associated with inside sales organizations. Ceilings are rising, and walls that once seemed impenetrable have been breached. Boundaries are blurring.

In other words, companies are raising thresholds at which inside sales groups can sell. The deal sizes are getting progressively larger among quota-carrying inside sales reps. Opportunities to travel outside of a corporate or centralized office location and meet with clients have also opened up. In some cases, the distinctions between inside and outside are eroding or disappearing. In some companies, there may be no ceilings on deal size and no wall-like restrictions on travel.

Blurring the Boundaries

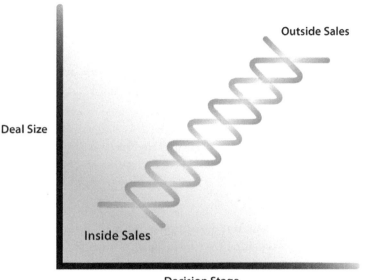

Source: *Visible Impact and Reality Works Group*

Companies are also relying on their inside sales organizations to test and open new market coverage areas. Areas that may have been unaddressed or underserved in the past are now prime targets for an inside sales organization.

This enables companies to be more agile in their market validation and go-to-market efforts. They can run experiments and explore new market opportunities. It offers them the ability to experiment not only in new markets, but to adapt quickly when they discover their hypotheses are incorrect or their go-to-market plans need refinement.

As Joe Bush, vice president of sales for TriNet, explains: "Inside sales is an optimal avenue for testing geographies, verticals and new go-to-market strategies. You want to successfully penetrate new or even underperforming markets. Inside sales allows you to do sample testing in multiple markets with little investment and in much less time. What would take you two years or more to figure out in a direct, field sales model, you can figure out in three to six months due to versatility and how you can analyze your market sample size."

With this approach, companies can explore "white spaces" and new territorial arrangements in an effort to drive growth and escape the margin pressures of today's intensely competitive markets. They can even grow globally in a more aggressive fashion and target emerging markets where demand and economic growth potential is higher.

Such initiatives simply aren't as easy to take on if your sales force is geographically bound and culturally oriented toward in-person meetings.

How Inside Sales Addresses a Weakness in Outside Sales

The inside sales model also addresses a demand that's long gone unmet in the sales profession. While salespeople are often portrayed as "lone wolves" who like to run their own territories, the reality is more complex. As humans, we all want to be part of a team. We want to share our challenges and successes with our peers. We want to learn from and even teach them. We want coaches and managers who will actively support our development. We want a strong sense that our careers are on solid and successful trajectories.

Field sales organizations, however, are struggling to meet these needs. They've become increasingly decentralized over time. Field salespeople are less and less likely to work out of regional or local offices. In fact, they are ever more likely to work from home, in airports and out of hotel rooms. They simply don't have the water-cooler opportunities they once had.

Inside sales is different. Generally speaking, inside sales involves a great deal of personal and team-oriented support. Because professionals in these organizations are typically co-located, ideas are actively shared, and the energy level can be quite high. The sense of being part of a team is often real and palpable.

Many inside sales organizations have their own cultures that are unique and separate from the rest of the sales organization or company as a whole. But their elevated level of excitement and team spirit can drive a positive culture shift across the entire organization. Organizations undergoing "sales transformation" or "culture shift" initiatives are, therefore, funding new or expanded inside sales initiatives. Some are even shifting head count from traditional sales roles to newly created roles with skills requirements associated with the best inside sellers.

Co-location offers an opportunity to accelerate and enhance skill development that's more difficult to accomplish with people in the field. When young professionals join an effective inside sales organization early in their careers, they develop habits and patterns that will serve them in future roles — whether those roles are in the field or in management or somewhere else in the organization.

They become effective time and process managers, as well as tool and technology users. They learn how to manage and capitalize on rapid information flows. They have time and stability in their day-to-day cadence that help them learn and develop. By contrast, field salespeople often have lives that are constantly interrupted by travel and transit demands. They are far less likely to get coaching, support and skill enablement on a day-to-day basis. Generally speaking, they are far more isolated and alone than their peers in inside sales organizations.

Repeatable, Predictable, Scalable

Consider the new "venture-driven" approach to selling. As previously mentioned, venture capitalists now expect their portfolio companies to embrace inside sales models. Executive leaders who value professional selling embrace the opportunity to engage prospects in a cost-effective way.

"The four founders of our company are a product expert, a design expert and two engineers," says Kevin Gaither, vice president of sales for ZipRecruiter. "They had no concept of sales organizations or sales models but, instead, focused on building a lean organization. Inside sales fit within that model, because it lends itself to a repeatable and predictable process. While a significant amount of our revenue comes from online channels, the investment in our inside sales reps typically pays off in 2–3 months. You can't say the same of outside sales reps."

As investor and consultant David Skok argues, inside sales is an order of magnitude less expensive to operate than field sales. While that may change in the years ahead (as field sellers adopt virtual selling techniques more aggressively), there is no question the cost profile associated with inside sales is far lower than the cost profile associated with conventional field sales efforts.[6]

Escalating Sales Expenses Tied to Resources

| Freemium | No-Touch Self Service | Light-Touch Inside Sales | High-Touch Inside Sales | Field Sales | Field Sales with SEs |

Rough Estimates of Customer Acquisition Cost (CAC)

| $0–$10 | $50–$200 | $1,000–$2,000 | $3,000–$8,000 | $25,000–$75,000 | $75,000–$200,000 |

Source: Matrix Partners

Companies that have fully embraced the inside sales model have experienced rapid and predictable growth. They have a revenue engine that's clear, manageable and scalable. Sales investments deliver visible and expected returns in a relatively brief time frame.

Other impressive outcomes include accelerated onboarding and enhanced professionalism, rapid ramps and reduced turnover. You can actively validate products and go-to-market initiatives at a time in which product life cycles are accelerating. And, by eliminating barriers that now confine inside sales teams, you can penetrate accounts and markets more deeply.

Whether you are targeting new verticals, geographies or buyer challenges, you have the resources to grow in new ways and at new levels.

What to Expect as Inside Sales Expands

The center of sales gravity is moving. As inside sales expands, you should expect to see a continuing investment shift.

Expect it in terms of organizational commitments. As research suggests, companies are now increasing their investments in inside sales relative to field sales. They are seeking the productivity and performance gains they see their peers and rivals experiencing all around.

Expect it in hiring as sales forces are reoriented, restructured and redesigned. Companies are realizing inside sales organizations can be talent factories. You can build a pipeline of talent for consistent performance over time.

Finally, expect to see more efforts to calibrate role definitions, territories and rules of engagement. While the ceilings are rising, and walls are falling in terms of inside sales, there will be more efforts to assess and determine where inside sales professionals and resources can deliver the best returns. Increasingly, the performance of inside sales is now measured beyond cost. Companies are looking at it in terms of strategic impact, predictability and overarching performance.

As buyers' demands and expectations change, you can engage them — virtually — in ways that once would have required lots of on-site, face-to-face interaction and lots of field sales support.

So why invest in inside sales? This is a strategy to increase growth and profitability. You can build a sales machine that you can actively monitor, manage and optimize. Your organization can learn more rapidly and act more decisively in its efforts to seize new market opportunities.

While the leaders of inside sales organizations often lack recognition, it's increasingly clear they shouldn't. All trends point to the growing application of the inside sales model across the board. Observant sales strategists and executive leaders are recognizing this pattern.

But inside sales doesn't operate in a vacuum. As we will discuss in the next chapter, the *Virtual Selling Imperative* represents new opportunities for field sales organizations, as well. Not only will professionals in outside sales increase their productivity and concentrate on more strategic deals, they will benefit from an influx of new talent that has been guided and developed by inside sales leaders.

Such patterns have important implications for sales organizations — inside and outside — going forward.

Strategy #3: The Outside Upside

It might seem that growing investments in virtual or remote selling come at the expense of field sales organizations. After all, when the growing role of inside sales comes up in conversation, it's not unusual for conventional field salespeople or managers to go on the defensive.

But they shouldn't. The reality is that the *Virtual Selling Imperative* represents an opportunity for you to take field sales organizations to new levels in terms of overall performance. There is an upside for those on the outside; this is the third strategy associated with Next Era Selling.

It's also time to cast a more discerning eye on the way resources are being deployed on behalf of field sales initiatives. In many companies, the numbers just don't add up. The cost of sales is simply too heavy relative to top-line contribution.

It's time for a rethink and a redesign.

But field sales isn't going away. On-site, in person meetings may become less common as time passes, but that just means these meetings must become more important and have more impact when they do occur.

What seems likely is tomorrow's field sales force will be better managed, supported, trained and capable of growing accounts than it is today. And, by leveraging the power of virtual selling techniques and approaches, outside sales professionals will become much higher performers.

What Separates the Outside from the Inside?

It's important to note at the outset that the lines between inside and outside (or field) sales are blurring. Where does one end and the next begin?

It is generally assumed an inside sales organization will be co-located in a shared physical space. That's not necessarily the case. You might have inside sales professionals who are widely distributed — even working from their homes. You might have someone designated as an inside salesperson who, nevertheless, periodically conducts in-person sales meetings.

Meanwhile, you may have field sales professionals who work from a centralized center or regional office. They may even sit right next to the inside salespeople.

There are all sorts of variations. But most field sales organizations are highly decentralized and highly distributed. Most outside sales professionals spend a lot of time operating on their own.

The virtual communication factor also isn't as much of a distinction as it used to be. Just like inside salespeople, many field salespeople spend an overwhelming percentage of their time on the phone, in a video conference, or engaged in digital interactions with prospects and clients.

Even compensation arrangements may not be a distinguishing point in some organizations. Both inside and outside sales professionals may carry sales quotas and have a high level of variable compensation, though, typically, field sales professionals have a larger variable component in their compensation mix.

What distinguishes the field force in most organizations is the high value associated with on-site, face-to-face meetings and the tendency to have fixed territories, typically based on geographies. Of course, other field salespeople may focus on key accounts, vertical industries or even particular parts of a product portfolio. But it's "the patch" they claim that makes them field or outside sales professionals — at least from a structural perspective.

Additionally, there is typically no ceiling on deal sizes field salespeople may pursue. What's increasingly interesting to explore is whether the minimum deal sizes, or floors, beneath them will begin to rise. If so, the deals they must pursue will take on a more strategic, less transactional cast.

Mounting Pressures on Field Sales Organizations

Sales leaders are now under pressure to keep a lid on sales expenses. We've seen increasing interest in the "S" in SG&A — the "Sales, General and Administrative" line on an income statement. CEOs and CFOs are now raising questions about sales expense to revenue (or booking ratios).

It's logarithmically (or 10 times) more expensive to sell through field sales than inside sales, according to Matrix Partners. So there'd better be either a way to justify that 10X variance in sales expense, or a way to throttle it back and make it merely a 5X difference.

This is playing out vividly in Silicon Valley, where companies have confronted the assumption that growth demands huge sales expenses. Some companies are now even built on the idea that expensive field forces are unnecessary and undesirable.

Rising Customer-Acquisition Costs

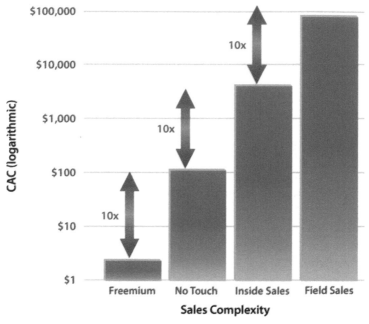

Source: Matrix Partners

The success of inside sales organizations is also putting pressure on field sales organizations to perform at new levels. Inside sales organizations have proved they can do deals on their own and carry sales quotas. They've demonstrated they can do deals of greater size and magnitude than ever before.

Interestingly, this perspective is filtering through the economy. Companies of all sizes are asking themselves how they might reduce sales expenses without sacrificing top-line growth.

One place this issue manifests is in sales travel expenses. Some might argue the first big blow to the field sales travel budgets came with the tech crash in the years right after the millennium turned. Not surprisingly, there was a great deal of interest in conference calls and web-based meetings as an alternative to meeting in person. The airline and travel industries took a hit.

The next big hit came with the financial collapse of 2008 and the Great Recession that followed. Once again, there was a reassessment of business practices and travel budgets. Some organizations changed their travel policies significantly.

Yet another trend reflecting on the current state of field sales is a slowdown in hiring — certainly a slowdown in relation to inside sales. Three inside salespeople are now hired for every field sales hire, according to InsideSales.com.

It's critical to recognize all these trends and patterns are ultimately grounded in the behavior of business buyers. The willingness of today's buyers to make more purchases and even bigger purchases through virtual interaction puts pressure on conventional field sales forces. And the increasing power of customers in today's intensely competitive markets is putting pressure on margins all around, particularly on field forces.

Conventional Sales Structures in the Crosshairs

So what's the current state? Conventional field forces are being scrutinized as never before. Many companies are simply dissatisfied with closing rates and lengthening deal cycles. Numbers aren't being met. Sales leaders are seeking higher performance and quota attainment.

There's also a drive to target new buyer roles, expand coverage areas and enter new markets. Companies are under pressure to move more quickly than ever to seize new market opportunities, and they've got to constantly be thinking about targeting new segments. But it's questionable whether field forces now lend themselves to such agile and rapid moves.

The field salesperson has traditionally been recognized as a sort of road warrior or big-game hunter. Indeed, there's romanticism associated with the entrepreneurial nature of the sales profession as practiced by field salespeople. They've been given a lot of autonomy over the years. If you met your quota, your autonomy was respected to a great degree.

There's been increasing encroachment on this autonomy. As CRM systems become more pervasive, and executives demand more detailed reporting, field salespeople are expected to enter more data and share more information. Even when you're making your numbers, much more attention is being placed on the data and descriptions you provide.

With this in mind, sales managers have acknowledged the existence of something they call "the last-mile problem." This problem reflects the fact that much field sales activity largely happens out of sight and beyond the influence of management. You can't manage what you can't see.

Sales leaders are increasingly hungry for data to drive predictable growth strategies. That's one reason field sales activities are now under active examination, while inside sales organizations are experiencing explosive growth.

According to a recent research report from ZS Associates and Reality Works Group, 40% of large high-tech companies intend to shift resources from field sales to the inside sales organization during the next two years. And while inside sales represents just 10% of revenue at large firms now (and so can expect to see a steep increase), it already represents 55% of sales at smaller, fast-growth tech firms.[7]

The difference? Field sales largely takes place "off the grid" (hidden from view), while inside sales work largely happens "on the grid" (where everyone sees what's going on).

The data generated when sales activities are tracked are used to analyze behavior, forecast outcomes and make performance-driving course corrections. So field sales is hampered by the fact that so much selling activity is not trackable or observable. While face-to-face meetings remain critical in many industries, the very fact that they happen off the grid helps explain why a sinking share of resources is now devoted to conventional field selling.

Another explanation for disappointing performance in the field may be excessive attention on sales work that might be described as transactional in nature. Unlike strategic deals that are large in size or represent big growth opportunities, transactional deals hold no such promise. While they may take less time to turn or effort to generate, it's questionable why you would want or need your most expensive sales team members devoted to producing them.

The implications or consequences of such arrangements are not pretty. When booking ratios are problematic, corporate profitability is at risk. What's more, companies are unable to adapt quickly as markets and buyer behaviors change. They are overly reliant on sales structures and territorial assignments that are difficult to change — even when sales coverage is deemed inadequate.

But the greatest risk is they will be unable to meet the demands and expectations of their best customers. That's the cost of spending so much time on transactional work. When strategic clients need more extensive guidance and support, field salespeople may be unable to provide it. In their pursuit of transactional deals, outside sales teams can miss out on strategic growth opportunities. They render themselves vulnerable to rivals who can provide superior offers and coverage in transactional situations, and rivals are prepared to go deep and act as true consultants in strategic situations.

Building a Talent Pipeline

Fortunately, there's an upside for field selling organizations — an Outside Upside. Your field team also has an opportunity to capitalize on the dynamics associated with the *Virtual Selling Imperative*. It's not an inside versus outside pattern; it's something on which all sales professionals can thrive.

Rather than resist this imperative, you must embrace it or be eclipsed by those who do. Some companies, for instance, have found the best performers on the outside were once among the best performers inside. As inside salespeople, they became masters of information flows and tool management. They learned to manage their time in a way that is far more aligned with the workflows and work-streams that now face field people. They've learned how to maximize virtual interactions to increase their productivity — even as field salespeople. They have brought with them advantages — such as faster responses to customers — that are serving them well as this next era plays out.

This is the single most important way that outside, or field, organizations are benefitting from the growth of virtual selling. It has enabled them to build a pipeline of talent, largely within their own organizations. When salespeople are trained initially in an inside sales organization, they develop a wealth of skills that can prepare them to be exceptional field salespeople.

They may have experienced the demanding cadence of a sales development professional, required to make or receive many calls and handle many email and social interactions. And they may have experienced the responsibilities of a quota-carrying inside sales rep whose targets are relatively transactional in nature.

When you promote these individuals to field sales roles, you'll find they have an array of valuable skills. For instance, they often bring with them an acute sense of how to invest their time for maximum results. This is nothing new in one sense. Great salespeople conventionally have been excellent managers of their time. But the accelerating and disorienting pace of today's business environment creates new time-management challenges to be considered and addressed.

At the same time, inside salespeople tend to be more analytical in their perspective on prospecting and customer engagement. They have been trained on managing a great many prospects and now, enabled with predictive analytics technologies, know how to prioritize them by value and propensity to make a purchase.

Joe Bush of TriNet explains that the inside reps who have gone to the field bring analytical skills that help them determine "where the propensity is to buy...it's easy for them to get data and capitalize on it." Not only do they have the stamina to handle demanding work, "they are conditioned to succeed," he adds. As a result, he's seeing reps move to the field and, on average, ramp up three times faster than existing reps and deliver productivity levels that are twice as high, all while demonstrating phenomenal levels of retention.

As this pattern suggests, there's an opportunity for successful practices being learned right now in inside sales organizations to be actively transferred to the field. Some of this opportunity could be seized through training, coaching and knowledge-transfer programs. But it also comes embedded in the people who are promoted to these roles.

Linda Connly, an AA-ISP board member and global sales leader at EMC, has experience with something she calls the "feeder model." Again, the idea is to develop salespeople within inside sales roles for about two years before presenting opportunities to join the field sales force. "We hire, create and cultivate talent, and we have a very clear career path," she says. "The model helps us create a seller that's going to have a new and different set of skills. This is going to really help transform our selling organization."

As Connly explains, new era sellers, who rely on virtual-selling skillsets and toolsets, have the ability to manage their territories in an extremely productive fashion. Even though they have field roles, they may actually work their patch in a far different way than prior professionals who've held these roles. "Our inside sales graduates are extremely efficient when they go to the field, because they're very disciplined in their prospecting," she says. "They realize how much they can accomplish via phone. They are wired that way and understand that you can be very productive through remote selling."

It's a different approach to field sales. "If this person sits in the office, they can have, easily, four scheduled calls. They can do demos, they can do whiteboards, they can do whatever they need to do," Connly says. "They're going to end up making way more money than if they're hopping in a car, trying to drive across their geographies. And so, it really does feel to me that this is how the sales force will evolve in the coming years."

The payoff so far has been significant. At EMC, inside sales graduates who've taken field roles out-perform, against quota, external field hires. And their attrition rates are nearly half the level of external hires. "We believe they tend to stay because we invest so much in them, and we create this bond of loyalty at an early stage in their careers," Connly adds.

Not surprisingly, the inside sales group at EMC has even been asked to train members of the field sales organization who haven't come from the inside. There's recognition, on behalf of the wider sales force, that virtual and remote selling skills are now a valuable asset for the field force.

Focusing on the Strategic Few

There's also a structural shift that's under way. As a growing number of companies have concluded, it's time to shift field salespersonnel to more strategic accounts and delegate transactional sales work to inside sales organizations.

This enables field salespeople to concentrate on key accounts or large accounts that represent extensive opportunity. When they focus on fewer, they can begin to see more patterns within these accounts — and issues of which even their customers may not be aware. They can become better advisers to their clients when they tighten their focus. They can identify more problems to solve and, as a result, cross-selling, up-selling and reference-selling become easier.

Going Upstream

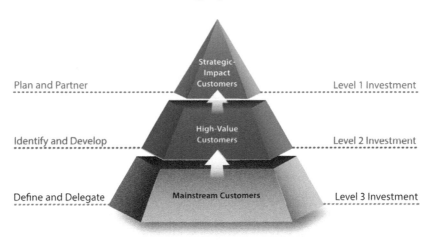

Source: Visible Impact and Reality Works Group

As account-driven professionals, they can point to existing successes within the account to create momentum and drive new growth. They can "land and expand" with far greater proficiency than they might have in an arrangement where their time is more thinly spread. (And, as we'll discuss in the next chapter, this capability can be even greater when accompanied by an inside sales counterpart and a team focused on account-driven marketing.)

While key account management is certainly nothing new, what is new is the need to redeploy field salespersonnel with an emphasis on strategic account development. Otherwise, you leave money on the table within existing accounts. You fail to solve problems your team is well-equipped to solve. Smaller, transactional opportunities, by contrast, can steal the field team's attention; they are a distraction, setting the stage for strategic opportunities to be seized by competitive rivals.

To execute this approach, sales force restructuring and redesign are necessary. Rather than treating geographical territories as open ranges for field salespeople to explore and exploit, it's now critical to make deeper distinctions based on sound analysis.

In Search of Expansion Revenue

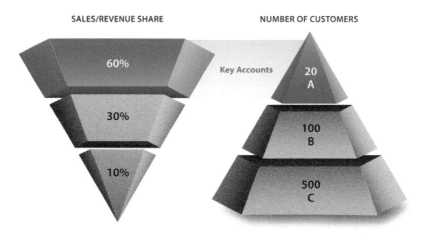

Source: Visible Impact and Reality Works Group

"We've seen it's possible to close the same or bigger-sized deals in a shorter period of time without all the extra expense associated with building in-person relationships with prospects," says Kevin Gaither, who leads sales at ZipRecruiter. "We recognize that this only applies to a transactional or a high-velocity sales cycle, but it's been the catalyst for creating a hybrid team consisting of 80% inside reps and 20% outside reps. The 20% focus on the upper echelon of buyers who want and often need us to go on-site."

While field salespeople generally have no ceiling on deal size or revenue they can generate within any given account, it's more interesting to consider the floor on which they stand. In other words, what is the minimum deal size for a field sales rep? The trend or pattern seems to be toward raising these floors significantly.

As such, field salespeople move their attention toward strategic accounts that represent substantial revenue potential going forward.

This can be a difficult transition on several fronts. It may mean the length of deal cycles will expand. Sales leaders and managers, in turn, will have to be more patient for field sales results. This may also be a difficult transition, at least psychologically, for many field salespeople. They may not get as many quick hits or morale-boosting sales in a given period of time. For many salespeople, turning deals brings excitement and motivation to their jobs. What happens when they turn far fewer of them (even when the ones they do close are larger than deals they closed in the past)?

Whatever the challenges of making this transition, many companies are making it, particularly larger incumbents. They are trying to strike a different balance between inside and outside sales groups. As a result, they are raising the ceilings over the inside teams and raising the floors under outside teams.

This redesign and restructuring is an indirect consequence of changes in the way buyers buy and the ability of suppliers to sell remotely. It allows companies to rely on their inside sales organizations to sell deals of progressively greater size and importance while redeploying the field team to still larger accounts. This makes sense. It's typically easier to grow and retain existing accounts than to acquire new ones, and existing accounts tend to be far more profitable.

This is happening at EMC. The customer size thresholds at which quota-carrying inside sales reps operate has progressively risen. Reps are even incentivized to push deals over those thresholds, which are generally determined by employee counts. That approach is designed to overcome the classic problem of reps trying to keep deal sizes under a certain threshold in order to retain their deals and count them against their quotas.

Getting on the Grid

The second element of this strategy is a move we describe as "getting on the grid." This means field salespeople must become more visible and collaborative on many fronts. While many professionals in these roles may have been largely on their own in the past, the future points to increasing interaction as the path to high performance.

What's more, salespeople will need to have more active and engaging relationships with their managers and field sales colleagues. Indeed, organizations are now taking steps to accelerate and enhance learning in the field. They are intent on enhancing performance management and feedback loops. To be off the grid is to be beyond the purview and perspective of the sales organization. This explains why sales behavior and performance has often been so difficult to improve.

In this new era, you can expect an increasing amount of attention to be placed on "social learning" and "sales huddles." Whereas training has often been treated as an event (often occurring around the annual sales kickoff), the best way to manage and enhance performance is through incremental, continual and iterative support.

Consider how coaches work with high-performing athletes: They provide active input and feedback to the performer. This is what companies are trying to achieve now. Virtual communication and collaboration now make it possible.

Sales teams can "huddle" periodically to share tips and tactics, practices and perspectives. "The purpose of a sales huddle is quite the opposite of a typical status and forecast meeting," explains Elay Cohen, founder of SalesHood and a former sales leader at Salesforce.com. "Instead of having teams classify their deals by pipeline stage, a sales huddle is a collaborative meeting that facilitates real-world learning where salespeople can practice new tactics and refresh old skills, and then apply these to active deals and scenarios with real customers. More importantly, sales huddles provide an environment in which salespeople can report back to their peers, and share how the new skill was used and to what effect. Their experience is shared, and feedback can be provided in real time, so coaching and mentoring becomes crowdsourced by the entire team."[8]

When these meetings are well-organized and managed, they can significantly add to a sales team's tribal knowledge. And, by capturing these events and recording them, you can create new digital assets that enable further analysis and support the skill development of new recruits.

Being on the grid also means deepening the connection between sales managers and sales reps. Time must be effectively invested in account strategy. By turning attention to fewer accounts, these conversations can become far more rich and relevant. Coaching and learning can have a deeper impact.

Rather than chasing many accounts with a transactional mindset, you can now focus on the strategic few — or, at least, fewer. Now, all members of the field team can get deeper into accounts and get a better handle on which moves might be made or explored.

It also will be necessary to involve more collaborators in actual sales calls. Unlike the "four in a box" type of approach once celebrated by companies such as IBM, you won't have a full set of team members engaged in an on-site, face-to-face client meeting and traveling together on the road. That kind of activity will become less common.

But you can involve other team members, such as product and industry experts, in on-site sales conversations, even when they cannot physically attend. These calls might even be recorded, enabling further analysis of potential opportunities. Widening the account discussion to other team members can surface opportunities that might not be evident to a field salesperson sitting across the table from a client or prospect.

By bringing other parties into these meetings, you extend the analytical capabilities that can be brought to bear in the assessment of account opportunities. You begin to address the last-mile problem. You surface tacit knowledge a rep may not always make explicit or fully express. By bringing sales conversations back on the grid and into a social, collaborative space, you create opportunities to make once-elusive opportunities tangible to the wider sales team.

This is one of the advantages inside sales organizations now have over field organizations. Team members can actively share their findings. They get far more feedback from sales managers and coaches. Sales interactions can be observed, recorded (with permission) and analyzed. The insights derived from these "visible" activities not only accelerate learning within the inside sales organization, they create opportunities to surface and seize new business opportunities.

It's now time for field organizations to capitalize on this dynamic. To do so, they have to bring their colleagues into their sales conversations and interactions. Even when they are sitting face-to-face with a prospect or client, they'll be wise to place their smartphone on the table, hit the "speaker" button or open their video conferencing application, and allow a colleague to participate.

Tending the Toolset

It's also apparent that organizations can strengthen field sales teams by enabling them to more fully capitalize on their tools, technologies and information flows. Much remains to be learned about how to maximize the value of sales toolsets.

New "sales acceleration" technologies are emerging every day with the promise of enhancing field performance. Recent data from CSO Insights shows field sales personnel are actually spending slightly less time using their CRM systems than they have in years past.[9] That might suggest the new tools are taking up more of their time. Or it could be a statement about sales force resistance to CRM tools. It's hard to say.

It seems self-evident, however, that sales organizations have much to gain by enabling and encouraging their field teams to perform better with their tools.

On this front, field forces may have much to learn from inside sales organizations. One inside sales advantage is workspace stability. Inside salespeople have their tools within their grasp every hour of every day. Unlike field salespeople, their days are not broken up by the demands of transit and on-site meetings. They can get far more adept at applying a certain set of tools, because they spend so much more time with them.

While field forces have tools that support greater mobility, there is a constant shift between a stable environment (such as a home office workspace) and a mobile environment (which may mean a plane, a coffeehouse or a customer's office). This puts the field salesperson at a severe disadvantage from a technology perspective. It's extremely difficult to manage all these tools and all the information flows associated with them when your days are loaded with disruptions. The work experience of a field salesperson is hardly seamless.

That means companies such as yours must guide and support field salespeople. You want to invest in the best productivity tools you can give them and train them for maximum impact. You can expect more and more sales conversations conducted by field sales professionals to involve a phone, a shared screen and other digital interaction technologies. That's good news. They will not only make more use of their limited time, they'll produce valuable data — the resource you need to amplify insight, learning and growth.

Virtual, Yet Personal

What's the upshot of these types of actions? Companies that are employing virtual selling practices to support their field forces are seeing early gains in terms of performance and profitability. They see the promise of higher retention among existing reps and faster onboarding of new reps. And, by enhancing and accelerating learning in the field, they are increasing the effectiveness of individuals and teams.

The biggest gains are likely to accompany greater strategic focus. Ultimately, they are capitalizing on "Pareto's Law," commonly known as the 80/20 Rule.

By enabling field reps to prioritize their relationships with the most promising and profitable accounts, you enable them to maximize growth. You encourage them to spend their time on the activities that will deliver the highest return for the business. You make it possible for them to act as true consultants and advisers by freeing them to focus their time on top accounts.

So inside sales and outside sales are not necessarily at odds, and the *Virtual Selling Imperative* need not be a threat. In fact, it represents an opportunity for inside and outside sales organizations to collaborate more assertively in the pursuit of growth. That's the approach we'll explore more deeply in our next chapter, which addresses a strategy we call the Inside–Outside Alliance.

Strategy #4: The Inside–Outside Alliance

As we've discussed, there's a specific upside for both inside and outside sales teams that successfully confront the *Virtual Selling Imperative*. But there's also an upside to be realized when inside and outside reps collaborate. Whether they are working together as "openers and closers" or collaborating as a team to sell into and grow accounts and markets, inside salespeople and field or partner salespeople have much to offer each other. Winning companies will commit themselves to exploring these angles, and adopt strategies and structures that are appropriate to their business models.

Too often, inside and outside sales teams operate in separate worlds, uninformed by the experiences of the other. But when they operate in silos, they miss the opportunities associated with synergy. They miss the chance to realize scale efficiencies or fully capitalize on their respective strengths. But this need not happen to you. By putting the right sales strategies in place, you enter the vanguard of Next Era Selling. Let's explore some of the ways you can drive profitable growth by building an Inside–Outside Alliance.

Trending Now: Sales Development

Sales efficiency problems are an extreme headache for many companies. In an era of escalating customer demands, heightened competition and excessive sales costs threaten the success of the enterprise. The leading indicators that matter most include factors such as selling time, pipeline volume and velocity, and sales cycle length. Sometimes, there's a mismatch between customer acquisition cost and customer lifetime value. You want to address concerns around these indicators in order to deliver and sustain impressive sales performance.

That's why it's so interesting that field salespeople — the most expensive quota-carrying reps — still spend so much time engaged in their own prospecting efforts. Reps, in other words, are pulled in many directions. They spend a lot of time on activities they don't like doing and aren't particularly good at performing. They may get wrapped up in transactional sales work that has no strategic or high value implications. This contributes to inefficiencies and resource misallocations.

However, the issue is attracting more and more attention at executive levels. During the past decade, there's been an enormous investment in "sales development" initiatives. Prospecting, lead generation, lead nurturing and appointment setting are being separated from the work of managing a deal. The trend has been particularly pronounced among high-tech firms that have embraced the possibilities associated with this new division of labor.

While insurgent companies in Silicon Valley and elsewhere seem to be aggressively adopting this approach, many incumbent organizations have been far less assertive on this front. Even many young companies have struggled to put in place the structures and systems necessary to thrive on this practice.

Companies that treat their sales forces in a traditional way tend to leave territorial reps on their own to build their own territories. They rely on lagging indicators — such as revenue performance and quota attainment — to measure the effectiveness of their reps.

Some don't actively monitor leading indicators — including the factors that create a strong pipeline — in relation to outcomes in the field. As a result, they have little ability to influence outcomes on a day-to-day basis. Too often, unqualified leads are handed off to sales. And too often, field reps are responsible for a large proportion of their own prospecting efforts.

Taking a New Direction

The implications are troubling. At a high level, sales inefficiencies mean companies are vulnerable to disruption by nimble competitors. You can't generate enough new leads and opportunities when you have no rigorous approach to outbound outreach. You can't fill sales pipelines when you have no systematic means of generating and nurturing leads. You are likely to suffer poor conversion ratios from lead to opportunity when you don't have an adequate means of qualifying prospects and moving them forward.

Ultimately, performance ratios — particularly revenue to sales expense — become deeply problematic when your company clings to outdated approaches to lead generation and pipeline development. You are unable to expand coverage areas or efficiently target new markets. By failing to free up your most highly compensated reps to pursue high-value deals with full focus, you can undermine growth at every turn.

That's why next era companies are dividing up roles and investing actively in sales development. This arrangement capitalizes on the economics of specialization at a foundational level.

It allows companies to deploy salespeople in clarified and defined roles that give them greater focus, satisfaction and success. And it helps companies produce critical gains around pipeline volume and velocity — gains that ultimately translate into growth and profit.

Standing Still: Implications and Consequences

When your company underinvests or fails to invest in advanced approaches to sales development, you magnify the misalignment that's all too common in marketing and selling efforts. You end up with an enormous amount of finger-pointing and blame-shifting.

What's that look like? It's typical for marketing to blame the sales team for failing to adequately follow up on the leads they've produced. Sales, in turn, will claim the leads are no good. As a result, marketing investments go nowhere, producing a terrible return.

Misalignment manifests itself in three key ways: misallocated talent, process inadequacies and low conversion rates. Consider these one by one:

1. Misallocated talent: Few would debate the proposition that it makes no sense to tie up highly paid professionals in work that is unmatched to their skillsets. Yet sales organizations do it all the time with field salespersonnel. They are often expected to spend a lot of time prospecting in order to help build their own pipelines. While a certain amount of prospecting is certainly sensible, the question is: How much?

All evidence suggests quota-carrying reps hate this activity and are poor at performing it when it involves a great deal of time and attention on their part. After all, it can take a great number of calls, emails and social media messages to simply get a prospect on the phone.

According to Vorsight, a sales training and demand generation firm, it can take 60–90 dials to set an appointment. How does that break down? It takes 12.73 dials to complete a call when a list includes direct phone numbers (18.83 dials when the list is based on switchboard numbers). It takes 22.5 dials to have a meaningful conversation (and sometimes as many as 30 when reaching out to prospects in highly solicited roles). Finally, it takes three meaningful conversations to get a single appointment.[10]

Those numbers are daunting to a field rep who is also responsible for conducting meetings, managing deals, negotiating and closing — not to mention all the reporting and administrative work that has become part of their job.

It's problematic to expect someone with so many other demanding responsibilities to also carry the load associated with prospecting and lead development. When companies make these added demands, they are simply misallocating resources and heightening the potential for disappointment.

2. Process inadequacies: While the dialing activity associated with lead development is certainly difficult to execute, the challenge of generating and nurturing leads is made still harder by other digital demands. To set an appointment or qualify a prospect, you frequently have to combine phone outreach with digital interactions, including email and social media touches. This multichannel factor, then, is one more reason sales reps are poorly equipped to build their own pipelines. It takes time, attention and a stable workspace to handle this heavy volume of communication activity. You have to manage not only a large number of outbound touches, but also a diverse mix of them.

It also takes persistence. You have to follow up actively and regularly to get your prospects on the phone. Random acts don't work. Nor does insufficient follow-up. In many cases, prospects are more than willing to have a conversation. They are simply unavailable at any given time. So it takes more effort to make a live connection or identify a time when a conversation can take place.

Yet another factor is the issue of response time. Industry research suggests the likelihood of converting a lead to an opportunity falls precipitously as time elapses. "If a company attempts phone contact within 5 minutes after lead submission, the odds that the lead is contacted are 100 times greater than if it is contacted 30 minutes after submission," according to research from InsideSales.com.[11]

It's virtually impossible to do this well when your role includes numerous other complex selling activities. Throw in the likelihood of travel and sales meetings, and the workload demands become impossible to meet. No single person can handle all these responsibilities.

3. Low conversion rates: It's one thing to execute the actions necessary to connect and converse with a prospect. It's still another to ensure a conversation is clarifying and qualifying. But leads and prospects must be qualified to achieve high conversions from lead to opportunity.

Failure occurs when marketing hands off unqualified leads to sales reps. That puts the onus on the rep to determine if the lead is genuine. In such cases, it's common for sales reps to simply ignore the leads. It's also common for them to spend a huge amount of time and energy engaged in their own efforts to qualify the leads. Both actions are inefficient.

You can't effectively and efficiently build a sales pipeline if you're depending on your quota-carrying sales reps to do all the work. It just won't get done. Why? Because it's harder than ever to engage prospects in a rich and rewarding dialogue — even when an existing relationship or personal connection exists. You are simply competing with too many other factors that are draining their limited time and attention.

Strategic Results through Collaboration

Up against these concerns and challenges, companies are now actively committing themselves to a sales development solution — a key element in the success strategy we refer to as the Inside-Outside Alliance. This can take on several forms. You might have inside reps generating leads and appointments for field reps, account-focused reps or even channel partners. Of course, you can also have sales development reps generating leads for quota-carrying inside sales reps — an increasingly common scenario.

For this strategy, the key factor in the mix is active and rigorous collaboration between inside and outside selling groups. In this case, the sales development organization focuses on enabling the field selling team to perform with far greater focus and effectiveness. By taking on responsibilities for lead generation, lead nurturing, lead qualification and appointment setting, sales development reps (SDRs) play a powerful role in opportunity and pipeline development.

To get there, you have to fund and build a sales development organization. You have to cultivate a cadre of inbound and outreach specialists. Their success involves a mix of activity and acumen. SDR teams need not be highly advanced in terms of overall work experience. It's common to have teams made up of young professionals who are recent college graduates, but in many cases, teams include entry-level sellers with no college degrees. What's most important is energy and enthusiasm, work ethic and professional drive.

They also need to be aggressive learners. They will be learning on the job, accumulating skills in customer communication, data and tool management, team collaboration, and time management. They must value and act on performance feedback. In many cases, their actions will be closely monitored, and their outcomes will be carefully tracked.

In the best organizations, their managers will be looking for leading indicators that clarify performance. Given the close connections SDRs often have with their managers, they may even receive guidance on a daily basis that enables them to continually improve and correct course.

Pursuing Opportunities as a Team

While some reps will be in inbound roles (responding to the actions and requests of prospects), others will be in outbound roles, actively reaching out to prospects that fit certain criteria. They will also be responsible for nurturing leads and following up with prospects to produce opportunities.

Openers and Closers

Source: Visible Impact and Reality Works Group

Ralph Barsi, who leads the global demand center at ServiceNow, notes the most significant source of sales collaboration in many firms involves "openers" and "closers." As he explains, the openers "schedule meetings with key folks that fit our ideal customer profile. They get the conversation started, and they get the company's foot in the doors of prospective accounts that we've got our eyes on." It's up to field sales reps, or account executives, to carry the deal forward and close it.

Outbound prospecting remains critical in this era — even as some marketing gurus claim that buyers can manage their own journeys. "You don't always have the privilege or the luxury of an inbound inquiry," Barsi adds. "Instead, you're knocking on the doors of prospective accounts, saying: 'We've learned quite a bit about you. We've been researching you. Based on the intelligence we have gathered, we think it might make sense to introduce ourselves at this point and see if you agree that it makes sense to start a discussion.'"

As Barsi sees it, there's virtue in being well-prepared and gathering sales intelligence if you want to be a successful opener. "We're going to measure twice and cut once," he says. "So, if we're going to call you, we're going to make sure that we know your business as much as we can and we have rationale behind why we're calling right now. We also want your buy-in on whether you think it makes sense at this time to talk. You've got to come to a prospect with a compelling reason and a compelling story as to why it makes sense to talk right now."

The approach works because there's a division of labor — a commitment to specialization. In the case of high-impact, complex deals, there's a significant amount of focused activity that needs to happen in order to initially qualify an opportunity and get meetings with key members of a decision team. And then, there's a lot of focused activity that's required once the opportunity is in play. You need specialization to win the deal. But you first need collaboration — an Inside-Outside Alliance — to make the deal possible.

The SDR Workflow

It's extremely difficult to manage the workflow now associated with generating and nurturing leads. It requires a high volume of focused activity that is contrary to the productivity of an outside rep. It involves interaction in multiple channels. And it involves application of data and technology in a way that is not possible when your work is constantly interrupted by travel, customer meetings, administrivia and account planning.

That's why sales development teams have stepped in to manage the lead management and even, in some cases, the account research process. Whether these activities are managed internally, outsourced or handled through a combination, you need dedicated specialists to handle this complex flow of communications, task management and lead research.

You need a stable workflow and steady cadence to operate in this way. You may be making more than 100 calls in a day. You may be leaving behind many voice mails. You may be managing numerous email interactions. You may be actively involved in social media.

To manage this level of activity, you typically need to be in one place for a great deal of time. And everything you do needs to be digitally trackable. You will be living in your CRM application and carefully recording every activity — though, of course, many actions are automatically recorded. You must be committed to the active management and refinement of data. It is, after all, the lifeblood of your work.

Just consider all the technologies involved in an SDR's daily workflow. There's the CRM or pipeline management application in which all customer data is captured and recorded. There may be a sales intelligence or predictive analytics application that enables you to make connections, build your list, ensure contact information is accurate, and profile your prospects. Turning to an application such as LinkedIn, you'll learn about a prospect's current role, job history and other personal factors that can bring relevance to your interactions and conversations.

You may use predictive technology that guides your reps to the right prospects and even suggests what to discuss in a given sales conversation. You may rely on an automated dialing system that facilitates outbound outreach and enables you to handle such extensive call volumes. You may use a sales email application that allows you to reach out to prospects on a digital basis, and even receive alerts when an email is opened or a link is clicked.

Meanwhile, managers may rely on a host of performance dashboards and technologies to track key indicators and ensure the team is on target. Guided coaching and guided selling technologies are increasingly applied to facilitate coaching, enhance knowledge transfer and accelerate learning. As a manager, you may listen to calls to track the skills, competencies and personal development of your people. By recording calls and recognizing typical scenarios, you can provide valuable learning resources for new recruits, as well as insights and best practices for the rest of the team.

This unique blend of data, technology, interactions, coaching and competency development — all woven into a fast-paced, high-intensity workflow and sales cadence — is what makes the SDR role so singularly valuable and necessary.

Measuring and Tracking Sales Development

Measurement and tracking are additional factors that facilitate the Inside–Outside Alliance.

You can't, for instance, manage leads effectively unless you have a sophisticated means of tracking their movement. You have to know when a conversion takes place. You need a clear definition of a lead as it is perceived and recognized by the sales reps who will act on it. In the absence of such clarity, there is misalignment. Sales reps will merely waste time following up on their own — something they are unprepared to do. Otherwise, they will dismiss the lead or give it scant attention.

This is how sales and marketing organizations come to distrust each other. Sales development organizations, therefore, are necessary to cultivate and qualify leads. They step into the breach, bringing marketing and selling teams back into alignment.

To ensure you remain on track in terms of managing this lead development engine, you have to stay on top of core metrics. It can be helpful to think in terms of activity metrics and outcome metrics.

Activity metrics enable you to manage the day-to-day operations of the sales development organization. With these measures, you can track and optimize the performance of your SDRs.

You are typically tracking activities such as calls or digital touches, responses, conversations, and qualified leads. You want to know the conversion rate from one stage of a buyer's decision cycle to another, to identify any bottlenecks or weaknesses. But you are also tracking other activities, including response rates from email and voice mail. Of course, it's critical to know what percentage of generated leads has been accepted by sales reps. Low acceptance rates suggest a need for intervention.

Meanwhile, outcome metrics help you clarify the overall effectiveness of your team. You can step back and track issues such as the impact of sales development on the sales pipeline (including the percentage of pipeline sourced by SDRs), the number of qualified leads produced by SDRs, and overall closed revenue tied to the sales development team.

By tracking such metrics in a systematic fashion, you clarify where performance gaps might exist and what actions are necessary to optimize the engine. However, you can't accomplish this objective when marketing is handing over unqualified leads and testing the patience of sales reps. When the deals are complex, successful lead development requires a dedicated team that is managing, nurturing and qualifying leads in a demanding environment where a great deal of phone and digital interaction is required.

Expanding through a Teaming Model

The Inside–Outside Alliance gives you additional opportunities and possibilities.

Some organizations have created special teams designed to collaboratively work specific territories related to geography, product or industry. In these cases, quota-carrying inside sales reps might team up with quota-carrying field reps to hit a specified revenue target.

Research from the AA-ISP recognizes a "teaming model" that brings a host of benefits: heightened collaboration, deeper product knowledge, and enhanced customer or market expertise. But challenges are sometimes associated with this approach, too. Among them: lack of accountability, lack of recognition, inconsistency among territories and difficulties measuring ROI.[12]

Shared Territory

Source: Visible Impact and Reality Works Group

In some companies, deals are switched from rep to rep depending on who makes the most sense to work the deal. In the best-functioning teams, the field team is freed up to chase large, unlimited deals, while their counterparts in inside sales ensure the existing customer base and the market coverage area is properly worked.

Gary Smyth, who has led inside sales teams for Oracle and now runs an Austin-based consulting firm called Sales Elite, discusses several of the dynamics in play in today's inside–outside partnerships.

"For sales organizations that have more of a focus on acquiring net new customers, it is not unusual to see territories structured based on geography as well as a prospect's annual revenue," he notes. "A territory may be composed of a state/large metropolitan area and prospects under a certain revenue band such as $100 million. The field sales rep would have a dual role: operating as the field sales rep located in-territory and also the manager of an inside sales team. The field sales rep would then own and be compensated on the quota for the entire region, with each inside sales rep owning and being compensated for his or her own percentage of the overall quota."

Smyth contends it's essential to have a "structured engagement model" that facilitates collaboration between inside and outside reps. For instance, the model at Oracle might include weekly meetings tied to measurable activities, quarterly "hub visits" that bring the inside and field teams together, and constant business reviews.

With a focus on professional development and building the brand for inside sales within an organization, "an inside sales showcase" can be a good tactic to build awareness of inside sales' strengths and leadership with a predominantly outside sales environment, Smyth adds. Senior field executives would spend the day with their respective inside counterparts to learn about go-to-market strategy and tools/technologies being leveraged. Benefits include a unified territory plan, additional career opportunities for the inside sales teams, and improved communication.

To avoid channel conflict and maximize territory coverage, opportunity thresholds by dollar value can be put into place, he says. The inside sales team, for instance, might focus on opportunity sizes of less than $100K in net new markets, and the outside sales team would focus on opportunities of more than $100K. Opportunities can then be reviewed on a deal-by-deal basis if they fall outside the guidelines. Some reasons for making exceptions: a customer satisfaction challenge or a requirement to be on-site to troubleshoot product issues. "For larger, enterprise-type accounts, a successful approach to territory management can be the field sales team focusing on the parent entity, while the inside sales team focuses on mergers, acquisitions, divestitures or subsidiaries of that parent account," Smyth says.

Coordination, meanwhile, is increasingly facilitated by CRM systems and other social technologies. Systems of this sort can ensure both inside and outside sales organizations are notified of opportunities in real time while avoiding duplication of efforts. Some companies may even have inside sales organizations teamed up with channel partners in an effort to extend market coverage in a scalable and cost-effective way.

Who's the Quarterback?

Still another possibility revolves around a reversal in terms of who is quarterbacking deals. While field salespeople conventionally have taken the lead in terms of deal and client ownership, it's increasingly plausible that inside reps might begin to take the lead. After all, the inside reps may have access to a much richer assortment of information and a much better workflow in terms of managing it. The inside rep, thus, has a much better vantage for strategic client management.

You could even imagine the inside sales specialists dispatching the field sales professional — or product specialist, sales consultant or local partner — to build trust and provide face-to-face support as necessary. The inside person would, in this case, play the role of client lead and deserve to be compensated as such.

While this may be the point where inside sales becomes indistinguishable from strategic account manager, it's nevertheless worth keeping an eye out for patterns of this sort. These days, there is a growing amount of interest in "account-driven" strategies. As marketers embrace "account-based marketing" approaches that begin with a highly targeted focus on specific accounts, strategic account management is more important than ever. Large or promising accounts become markets unto themselves.

Contrary to the high-volume approaches associated with much of sales development today, you can expect to see account-driven approaches that require inside and outside sales specialists, as well as account-focused marketers, to work together to make big accounts even bigger.

As business strategists have long noted, it's easier and more profitable to grow existing customer relationships than it is to develop new ones. Expect to see more attention placed on this core principle of growth in the coming years. It will require account teams to generate more insight and situational awareness so they can approach their customers with deeply relevant messages, hypotheses and solution options. They will focus on value, not volume.

Capitalizing on the Inside–Outside Alliance

ADP, a market leader in payroll and human resource management solutions, has deployed the team model in multiple ways. While quota-carrying, inside sales reps have discrete territories in some cases, they collaborate within territories in other cases.

"We have a wide variety of programs," says Liz Gelb-O'Connor, a senior ADP leader who has overseen inside sales strategy and social selling. "We found that, in some cases, a team model is one of the best models. We work in tandem as a team within large accounts, and then divide and conquer, and basically extend our activities and appear to be more coordinated in the eyes of our clients."

Team arrangements sometimes involve inside reps selling different products from their outside counterparts within the same accounts. "Rather than having our field partners getting bogged down in smaller sales, the inside sales team frees them up to pursue more complex deals. That's a key focus for us in the upper end of the market. They figure out a rhythm among themselves and do account plans together to meet their objectives," Gelb-O'Connor says.

Shared Account

Source: Visible Impact and Reality Works Group

This level of camaraderie was established within the past 3–4 years, which went a long way in resolving channel conflict between inside and field sales reps, and created a more optimal client experience.

"When we moved to this model, conflict went away almost overnight," Gelb-O'Conner says. "We started building good, trusting relationships, and all of a sudden, leads that we never had before were coming out of the woodwork. The inside reps were simply given more access into a wider range of accounts. Part of it was proving that we could manage and close more complicated deals."

So what was necessary to make this teaming model work? It was certainly critical to clarify the benefits that would be experienced in the field organization. But it was also vital to develop a new compensation arrangement that ensured everyone was rewarded for their contributions to new deals.

"Quota-stacking" ensured both inside and outside reps were compensated for deals within shared territories, which was more than justified by increased sales volume. Indeed, the results were extremely impressive. Sales expenses drop for numerous sales activities, and quota-crushing outcomes became increasingly common.

Forward Together

Where some might see brewing conflict in the interests of inside and outside sales teams, the larger picture is one of complementary strengths. Going forward, strategic sales leaders will recognize and seize upon the opportunity to maximize profitable growth by capitalizing on the unique capabilities of each organization.

It's no longer a game of alphas and betas, lead and support, or high and low prestige. Great careers are now made across the sales spectrum, and a full set of specialized talents must be brought to bear by today's executives and sales leaders to win in today's demanding markets. With this in mind, we'll now turn our attention to a strategy we call "Networked Specialization."

Strategy #5: Networked Specialization

As ecosystems evolve, they become more rich, varied and diverse. Organisms naturally seek ecological niches that set them apart from rivals and enable them to flourish. Economies are similar. Companies that operate in them perpetually seek a competitive advantage and organize with this in mind. They must specialize to differentiate themselves and drive growth.

And that's true for individuals, too. People naturally strive to be distinct in their professional lives, to offer unique and differentiated value. Companies harness these diverse talents to provide distinctive value and scale up to new levels.

Buyers, in turn, want added value or a unique experience. They expect more and more for the money they spend. In the B2B arena, they are increasingly likely to seek sophisticated guidance to facilitate complex decisions and implementations.

It's a feedback loop of sorts. Buyers expect more guidance, support and value for their dollar. Sellers provide more guidance, support and value to differentiate themselves.

This leads buyers to expect still more.

These are some of the reasons specialization now matters so much. The challenge revolves around delivering increasingly compelling and streamlined experiences when buyers also are resistant to cost increases. You can't just raise your prices to cover the cost of expert-level talent.

To overcome this challenge, you'll need to take a close look at how specialists of various kinds are being deployed in an increasingly virtual and networked selling environment. There are opportunities to capitalize on the centralized nature of inside sales talent, as well as the distributed nature of outside teams and other types of sales experts. When specialists are networked, it turns out, you have an opportunity to provide deepening expertise without an explosion of sales expenses.

Indeed, there are numerous advantages associated with using specialists in a virtual selling environment. Not only do you gain access to a wider spectrum of experts and make it possible to engage an audience spread out in disparate locations, you can contain or reduce costs.

Unmet Needs, Increasing Expectations

Step back, and consider your objective.

You're intent on meeting customers where they are in a decision cycle. Sometimes, they aren't very far along at all, but increasingly, they are well-informed. The reality, however, is they need more guidance than ever in a complex, high-stakes sale. If they are merely trying to inform themselves by downloading materials from the Internet, then they risk running into all sorts of unexpected traps.

This is where specialization becomes particularly critical. You want to provide the right resource at the right time to guide your buyer through a demanding decision.

You want to sell higher in an organization in order to accelerate your sales cycles. But that means you need to ensure you have the credibility to seek and gain executive access. You want to make existing accounts bigger. But that means you have to engage in account planning, and determine the right resource at each stage of a decision. You want to penetrate new markets. But again, you'll need to demonstrate you have the credibility to speak to new buyer concerns. You also need to address the concerns of technical influencers on the buying team. For that, you need specialists who bring deep technical expertise in analyzing implementation and integration issues.

As your outside salespeople redirect their energies toward increasingly strategic accounts, the demands they face surge. They are challenged to look at their accounts as markets unto themselves. That means there may be an extensive network of potential buyers and influencers within a single account who have different needs and interests and perspectives. They need the guidance of specialists who can speak to their particular concerns.

And as your inside salespeople take over a wider set of opportunities and geographies, inside sales organizations will depend on a wider set of skills. They'll need inbound lead managers, sales development specialists, lead researchers, inside sales reps and, of course, managers. While many buyers have relatively transactional needs that demand limited support, still others have more extensive support needs that will require the expertise of sales engineers or channel solution providers.

What's Wrong with the Present State?

In the absence of a specialized selling team, several key challenges are likely to surface:

Inability to sell at the right altitude: What every experienced sales manager understands is that you need executive sponsorship to accelerate a decision-making cycle. By no means is the senior decision-maker acting alone. But you need access to these high level buyers or influencers to maximize your success. Otherwise, you are always running uphill, struggling to get to the altitude of executives.

While one reason executives are reluctant to meet with salespeople is they don't expect them to have the business acumen necessary for valuable conversations, a greater issue may be perceptions of status. Executives are far more likely to meet with individuals they consider to be peers or experts of some sort — specialists who bring them immediate value and perspective.

How do you get executive access when your salespeople — inside or outside — lack the status necessary to engage these key stakeholders?

Unaddressed buyer concerns: Deals can also be impeded when the concerns of key stakeholders go unaddressed. That may be the chief financial officer or some financial executive. It may be a chief information officer or some key decision-maker responsible for information technology decisions.

Look at it this way: When engaged in a complex and demanding buying decision, every buyer has strategic, operational, financial and technical concerns. These factors can become a wall — even an impenetrable one — to break through if you are unprepared as a seller. If you can't credibly and convincingly address the issues that matter most to various stakeholders, the sales process is likely to stall at some point.

You need specialists, experts and thought leaders to get through these barriers. Sometimes you need to involve your own senior executives — top leaders who carry the status and can speak the language of the executive buyers you are trying to influence.

It's not just individual stakeholders deciding on their own whether to endorse a deal. One of the greatest challenges sales reps must address is driving consensus among various stakeholders. But your salespeople will need the input and expertise of specialists to build confidence with these stakeholders.

The overburdened sales rep: Top performers find a way to capitalize on their strengths and delegate or diminish activities they consider to be weaknesses. They are extremely focused and at their best when they reach a state the psychologists call "flow."

It's hard to reach this level when you are pulled in many directions and burdened with many low-value activities. That's what's happening to too many sales reps today, particularly those in the field.

Much is being asked of them in terms of prospecting, selling, data collection and administrative work. But these professional demands are not well-aligned with the sales objectives placed upon them. Perhaps it's unsurprising, then, that research firm CSO Insights finds CRM usage is declining among field reps. They simply lack the bandwidth to track all their activities.

Unlike inside sales reps, field reps rarely have the ability to spend a whole day in front of multiple digital screens. Their work lives are fragmented by travel and face-to-face meetings. That makes it difficult to manage increasingly voluminous information flows.

Such factors detract and distract reps from engaging in the work they are primarily hired to do. As a result, their morale, productivity and performance all suffer.

What are the top two issues undermining sales effectiveness today? According to a survey of senior sales executives by research firm SiriusDecisions, they are:

- Inability of reps to connect offerings to client business issues (71%)
- Reps spend too much time on non-selling activities (65%)

Companies now need to rethink both the way they engage their prospective clients and the burdens they place on salespeople. Networked Specialization, a fifth strategy associated with Next Era Selling, offers an opportunity to confront and surmount these difficult barriers to sales effectiveness.

Specialization Deepens as Virtual Selling Increases

What is Networked Specialization, and why does this represent a powerful strategy in the face of the *Virtual Selling Imperative*? After all, mature sales forces have always had specialists. Field reps are quite comfortable with bringing sales engineers and sales consultants — industry, product and technical specialists — into the selling process.

What's changed is buyers are more demanding than ever. They want more guidance. They want, in many cases, deeply tailored solutions that match their specific circumstances. They are dealing with more complexity and want more risk mitigation. They want more evidence. But that doesn't mean they are necessarily willing to pay more for all these "value-added" services.

How do you respond as a business or sales leader? You are challenged to deploy an increasingly skilled and diverse set of specialists to address escalating demands and expectations. But you can't afford to put those people in the field in every case. In fact, on-site field deployment is declining, even as the deployment of experts in the sales process continues to grow.

What makes specialization possible is sophisticated collaboration and communication technology. It allows you to deploy the right person at the right time to meet a buyer's need. It allows you to provide a great wealth of expertise, even as you transcend barriers of cost, time and geography.

Further, you can deploy them on-demand at the point and moment of need. You need not build a team of experts and run the risk of them sitting on the bench at great expense. That's what happens when expertise is rooted in a geography. But when experts can be deployed virtually from anywhere in the world, their location is practically irrelevant. For all intents and purposes, they are available on-demand. Of course, when an in-person visit is a requirement, partners or sales consultants located near a customer or prospect may be called upon to work in conjunction with a virtual seller or account manager from headquarters or another location.

The specialized selling team can be composed in different ways.

It can include client experts, vertical market specialists and thought leaders within your organization. Such individuals can help a buyer clarify the case for change and investment. They can help you sell at a higher level and open doors that might otherwise have remained closed.

The team can also include solution, product and technical experts. They help the buyer scope out the parameters of a potential solution and clarify how it can be implemented successfully. They consider issues of integration and user adoption.

You may have subject-matter experts who specialize in building the financial business case and running scenarios that demonstrate return on investment, total cost of ownership or annual rate of return. Companies such as SAP, Oracle, Workday, IBM and Salesforce.com have teams engaged in value engineering — building business cases that clarify and project business value.

To engage early-stage buyers, you may have sales or business development specialists. They take on prospecting and lead qualification responsibilities that require a great deal of focus and persistence. But you also need experts behind the scenes. That may include individuals who analyze markets, build lists, conduct client research or handle administrative activities that otherwise would fall on the shoulders of the quota-carrying rep. Deal desks, for instance, can play a key role in the development of proposals and the adjudication of terms.

Customer success specialists also are increasingly important. They help onboard new customers and ensure they have a positive experience that reflects the ROI they anticipated. In an economy in which switching costs are lower than ever, these roles are essential if suppliers are to maintain customer loyalty and a high customer lifetime value (CLV) relative to customer acquisition cost (CAC).

Specialization is deepening in many companies. However, it's the virtual connections that bind a networked company that make new levels of specialization economically feasible. The growing demands of buyers and heightened competition from rivals make it altogether necessary.

Want Executive Access? Enter the Statusphere

Want more conversations with decision-makers and influencers at senior levels? Want to engage the people who have the authority to sign your agreements and accelerate your sales cycles? Then you'll have to enter the Statusphere.

Consider the perspective of celebrated author and journalist Tom Wolfe, a keen observer of the status anxieties and ambitions that motivate human behavior.

In his book, *The Right Stuff*, he wrote about the status hierarchies associated with military pilots, suggesting astronauts were by no means at the apex of this highly competitive pyramid.

In *Bonfire of the Vanities*, he addressed the challenges facing social strivers in 1980s Manhattan.

In *Back to Blood*, Wolfe's latest novel set in Miami, he addresses the status struggles of Cuban-Americans, Russian plutocrats, Haitian immigrants, wealthy patrons of modern art, a psychiatrist focused on porn addiction, a Yale-educated editor of the *Miami Herald*, a mayor and a police chief.

"I think every living moment of a human being's life, unless the person is starving or in immediate danger of death in some other way, is controlled by a concern for status," Wolfe says.[13]

While he may be exaggerating a bit, he's essentially right. Every time someone requests a sales meeting, senior decision-makers ask themselves this: Should I take this meeting? Does this person rise to my altitude? Status concerns influence that decision.

Of course, sales managers are always telling salespeople to call higher. Underperformers are likely to get an earful in this regard. They are pressured to get senior-level access, and perhaps, go all the way to the top. They should. "When I look at the largest transactions ... every transaction was done with the CEO," said Salesforce.com CEO Marc Benioff.[14]

It's not an easy accomplishment. After all, senior decision-makers and influencers seek a status match. They are typically unwilling to meet with or take calls from someone perceived to be of lower status. To do so is to diminish their own perceived sense of status. (To be fair, it may be a waste of time anyway. According to Forrester Research, 85% of executives say sales meetings don't live up to their expectations.)[15]

It may not be politically correct to acknowledge this reality, but it's the truth. You don't get executive access unless you are perceived as a peer or a valued adviser.

What's the Solution? How do You Get Access?

One way to get access is by leveraging the status of your most senior executives. That means setting up meetings by deploying C-level leaders, whether it's your CEO, CFO or CMO. Startups often heavily rely on their founders to get access and make their initial deals possible. But it isn't just startups.

"These are CEO-level conversations; we're in the boardroom, presenting to the board," says Salesforce.com COO Keith Block, explaining his own involvement in the sales process. "In the past three weeks, I've had more conversations with CEOs around transformation than in my entire career over 30 years."

If you are looking to make a peer match, you can put people together who speak the same language and are experiencing the same sorts of challenges.

The problem? This approach doesn't really scale. Your executive leaders have a responsibility to lead. While they can spend a lot more time engaged in client conversations than they probably do, there is a limit to how much you can deploy them. Their time and availability is constrained.

That's why you want to build a team of dedicated thought leaders and trusted authorities — specialists or subject-matter experts in other words — within your organization. You can deploy them up front in the decision cycle to get access to senior people.

As thought leaders, they can be perceived as high-status figures if you build them up as such. You can use assorted subject-matter experts, market strategists and solution architects to establish this kind of credibility and convey valuable insight in a decision cycle. They may be provocateurs, even visionaries, within their realms of expertise.

Engage Senior Decision-Makers with Insight Selling

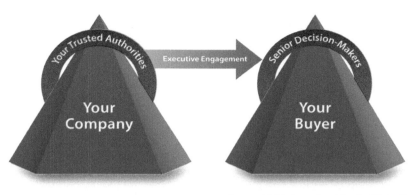

Source: Visible Impact and Reality Works Group

One company that pioneered this approach is strategy consulting firm McKinsey. It's a firm whose consultants publish and speak extensively, establishing a door-opening position as thought leaders. "It's the general principle of demonstrated competency rather than claimed competency," says Paul Friga, author of *The McKinsey Mind*. Other consulting firms, such as Bain and Boston Consulting Group, have since produced models and frameworks that define business thinking on certain topics.

It's increasingly common for companies of all types to draw on thought leaders to generate new frameworks and challenge the status quo, engage senior decision-makers and accelerate deal cycles. One example is Russell Glass, head of products for LinkedIn's Marketing Solutions group. He's the author (along with Sean Callahan) of *The Big Data-Driven Business*, an accomplishment that helps LinkedIn open doors and establish credibility in the marketing arena. Or take Cory Munchbach, once a star marketing analyst at Forrester Research, who was recruited by BlueConic, a fast-growth player in customer data management, to strengthen its thought leadership and engage in senior-level client meetings.

Executive leaders are often quite interested in meetings that promise to make them smarter or clarify issues critical to their success. However, they don't expect generalist or geo-based sales reps to have this level of expertise. To a great extent, they are right.

That said, sales reps can continue to play a critical role in the process by facilitating the decision as it moves forward. They will merely rely on their C-level execs, thought leaders and subject-matter experts to open doors on higher floors and move the decision forward at key points in the process.

By selling at a higher level, you can accelerate the decision-making cycle. You can overcome the no-decision problem and close more deals. But to get that opportunity, you need access. You need to enter the Statusphere. Your thought leaders can get you to the right altitude.

Addressing Complex and Technical Buyer Concerns

While your executives and thought leaders can help you address strategic buyer concerns in relation to why they should buy/change in the first place, a host of other concerns will emerge before a high-stakes decision is made. You also have to consider the financial, operational and technical dimensions of a solution: This is where a series of other stakeholders can be expected to weigh in.

Again, you'll need specialists to address buyer concerns and decision criteria. Operational, financial and technical stakeholders are often highly concerned with managing risk in its many guises. They have to make a judgment from their various vantages.

Financial stakeholders want to understand the financial risks and expected outcomes associated with an investment. They are particularly interested in the business case as it concerns matters of cost, payback periods and investment returns. In some cases, you'll want to deploy experts who can walk them through financial models that express business value quantitatively.

Avery Lerner, vice president of enterprise accounts at Oracle, is responsible for bringing financial acumen and quantitative expertise to major deals. Representing the company's finance division, he supports front-line salespeople and their clients in the development of the business case.

"We are a virtual part of the sales organization," Lerner says. "We talk finance with the customer. We discuss the return on investment and payback period [associated with a solution]. We do a lot of homework, try and analyze what's going on in the customer's financial statements, and speak the language of the CFO."

Technical stakeholders are also critical to deal success. They'll want to know what it takes to implement a solution from a technical standpoint and clarify issues around integration with existing systems and platforms. In the IT arena, some companies employ "enterprise architects" or other master strategists to scope out and define opportunities in terms of the buyer's technology roadmap.

It's also very common to deploy "sales engineers" (sometimes called "sales consultants" or some such) to define needs and demonstrate solutions, then collaborate with buyers on implementation and integration. What's changed in recent years is the tendency to handle more and more of this technical sales work at a distance. "The remote demonstration is now an increasingly important tool in the sales engineering arsenal," write John Care and Aron Bohlig in *Mastering Technical Sales*.[16]

Obviously, deals can quickly get beyond the expertise or bandwidth of a typical field or inside sales rep. That's why specialists matter so much.

What's changing is the increasing demand for special expertise. It's not that it didn't exist before; it clearly did. It's just a matter of degree. If more stakeholders are involved in a decision on the buyer's side, then it's likely more specialists must be deployed on the seller's side.

This is where the virtual factor comes into play. It's the only way to deploy these experts in a timely and cost-efficient manner. It's expensive and logistically challenging to fly experts to a buyer's site on a regular basis. Buyers don't want this, and you don't want this. Instead, you can facilitate a matchmaking of specialists with stakeholders — and do so increasingly through virtual communication and collaboration media. Your people can address key concerns in a just-in-time fashion. They can have rich interactions with decision-team members simply by using a phone, a webcam and a shared screen.

Unburdening Your Sales Reps

As we discussed, sales rep productivity and performance is undermined by overburdening their roles. By this, we mean that reps are expected to take on many tasks that are contrary to their major objective of revenue production. It's the challenge of sales organizations, and more specifically, sales support teams, to increase the capacity of quota-carrying and customer-facing reps.

The opportunity to efficiently delegate and disperse sales tasks is greater than ever in this virtual era. The question is how to define what is essential in a given sales role, and what can be offloaded to enhance overall sales performance and sales team outcomes.

Companies such as Iron Mountain, a leading player in the records management and data protection industry, have learned through experimentation and experience how to shift the load in ways that deliver tangible rewards_and payoffs. Recognizing reps were spending more than 20% of their time on back-office administrative work (compared to 27% engaged in customer contact), the company launched a sales support project it called "the sales factory." By relieving salespeople of tasks such as data aggregation from multiple systems, running specific reports, developing pricing models and new account setup, a team of 10 sales support coordinators was able to free up capacity for a sales force of 400.

In its evaluation of the program, Iron Mountain identified a perceptible savings of time per rep of roughly 4 or 5 hours per week. The biggest gains came to the middle 50% of sales rep performers. Visible improvements in quota attainment were correlated with active usage of the support service. What's more, reps provided feedback pointing to the impact on morale and motivation associated with delegating tedious tasks. Meanwhile, sales recruiters actively promoted the company's efforts to support and free up the sales team in their efforts to attract new talent.

As this example shows, sales organizations can strengthen performance in many ways by considering what activities might be unbundled from the sales rep's conventional job. By freeing your reps to focus on customer-facing activities, you enhance their ability to perform and deepen their connection to you as an employer.

Among the activities companies should consider delegating to enhance sales capacity:

- **Sales Development.** Among the greatest distractions from productive work are the challenges of educating early buyers, prospecting, appointment setting and lead qualification. Today's immense and growing interest in sales development reflects the necessity for specialization on this front. It's a demanding activity that requires the focused work of a specialist.

- **Account Research and Analysis.** To ensure reps are engaging prospects in compelling conversations, they need to have a clear and comprehensive understanding of the accounts they are seeking to penetrate. With thoughtful research and analysis, they can engage buyers with insights and perspectives that make them a valued consultant.

- **Back-End Administration.** There might be all sorts of challenges associated with assembling proposals, clarifying pricing options and vetting contracts. Such matters can slow down and even impede deals if they are not efficiently handled. By taking this burden off the sales reps, you give them more time for customer engagement while reducing needless stress.

- **Sales Technology Support.** Given the growing number of tools available to inside and outside reps, it's important to ensure they can manage this toolbox in an efficient way. By providing appropriate technical support, you ensure technology becomes a multiplier instead of a source of distraction. Email automation tools, for instance, can reduce the burden of repetitive tasks and enhance customer communications.

While there are many other possibilities, the point here is that the virtual interaction of dedicated specialists within a sales organization can enhance morale and performance. Today's systems enable us to define, sequence and coordinate sales work in increasingly dynamic ways. In a networked enterprise, work can be unbundled, and specialization can be embraced to achieve higher aims.

Collaborating as Complexity Intensifies

As the sheer complexity of a buyer's decision grows, it becomes ever more important for account managers and sales specialists to collaborate effectively. But they'll also need to consider the challenge of collaborating with their customers. According to research from Corporate Executive Board, buying-decision teams have an average of five or more stakeholders on them. In some cases, the number of stakeholders and influencers is even higher.[17]

On the supplier's side, you may have multiple specialists of various kinds who must collaborate to clarify a problem, design a solution, put together a proposal, and address all customer needs and concerns along a decision path. As a result, your sales rep or account manager can become a bottleneck in the process. When stakeholders on the buying team can't promptly get the answers they need from specialists in your organization, deals can get held up or even collapse altogether.

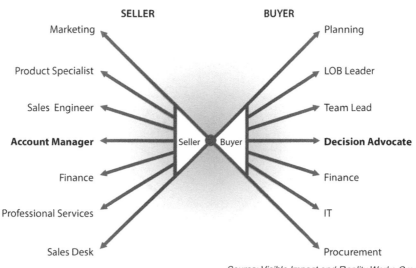

Bottlenecked Specialization

Source: Visible Impact and Reality Works Group

This need not be the case. Increasingly, companies are relying on social technologies to facilitate collaboration in a customer decision cycle. Robert Racine, vice president and global head of sales enablement at Wipro, describes his company's approach: "We implemented something we call 'auto communities.'"

As he explains, when his company is pursuing a large opportunity, it employs a system that creates "something like a Facebook for the deal. It plugs in all the people involved in the deal, so they can share knowledge, insights, and documents. They can collaborate by having three or four people working on the proposal at the same time, seeing each other's edits and being able to provide feedback. That level of digitization will produce huge advantages in terms of productivity and efficiency."

Such approaches can enable all parties — on both supplier and buyer sides of the equation — to work together in a highly visible and coordinated fashion. Where once there were barriers to impede discovery, design and solution discussions, now all parties can operate in parallel and in a shared online space.

As such, they can surmount barriers of time, availability, expense, organization and geography. In this increasingly complex environment, specialized selling teams and specialized buying teams can work together to make high-stakes deals far more successful.

Networked Specialization

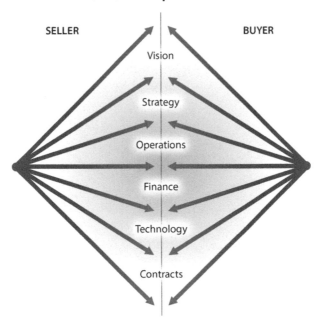

Source: Visible Impact and Reality Works Group

Consider an example shared by SAP's Anthony Leaper, senior vice president of enterprise social business. While working a large deal with an airline headquartered in the Gulf states, he and his team demonstrated what a powerful role the firm's own social collaboration technology, known as "Jam," could play in the customer engagement process.

With Leaper in flight and offline for nearly a dozen hours, specialists on his team fielded a series of buyer requests for business projections, technical specifications and information on other matters.

Here's where Jam had a significant impact. As opposed to a flurry of fragmented emails and calls, virtually all communications were now visible and accessible, housed in a collaborative space that made it clear who was participating in the deal (on both sides), what requests were being made, who was responding and what was getting accomplished.

When Leaper finally arrived at his destination and went online, he learned how far the deal had progressed in his absence. When he met with the company's decision-makers that day, his team's speed and thoroughness was immediately cited as a reason for moving forward. "We won the deal largely because of the agility and responsiveness of the team," he says.

SAP has taken this idea beyond the realm of technology. It recognizes that productivity and performance are often undermined when processes are ad hoc, business systems are fragmented, and expertise is disconnected from the challenge at hand. With this in mind, it has married collaboration technology with a concept it calls "work patterns."

Work patterns go beyond mere collaboration, putting social interaction in the context of particular types of work or business processes. To enable sales organizations, there might be work patterns around account management, deal support or customer engagement. Other SAP work patterns relate to employee onboarding, training and coaching, and channel support.

In terms of virtual selling and buying, such approaches remove friction, facilitating communication and collaboration, while ensuring key customer priorities, issues and concerns are surfaced in a visible and addressable way.

Even in a highly distributed environment, you can draw on your team members in a responsive, coordinated and cost-effective way. "You can increase the likelihood of deal success by enabling agile teams," Leaper says. "You can discover and leverage the value in your entire organization to support deals. And you can connect your customers to the people and information that can add value."

Specialize without Sacrifice

Companies cannot address the escalating expectations of their customers when they are reliant on an expansive army of sales generalists. Instead, they must specialize to an increasing degree. But they must figure out how to accomplish this task in a cost-effective manner if growth is to be profitable.

Up against these seemingly conflicting demands, Next Era Selling organizations have found a solution: networked specialization. They are accessing and deploying their specialists without necessarily requiring them to get on a plane or even travel across town. They are leveraging the power of new practices and advanced communication technologies, running their enterprises in a highly productive fashion, while giving customers the specific guidance and support they seek.

Conclusion:

Rebalancing Your Sales Investment Portfolio

Strategic thinking is critical. It helps ensure you are moving in the right direction — taking the right actions and making the right investments — as opposed to simply running very fast in the wrong direction. Herein, we've identified five strategies that will enable success in the next era of selling. By executing on these strategies, you position yourself to make your number — and win.

This executive briefing book was designed to present these strategies at a high level. It may prove challenging to meet your objectives and implement such strategies. And execution requires you to operate on multiple levels.

In a forthcoming sequel to this book, we'll explore several dimensions or design factors associated with a high-performance sales operation. Among them:

- **Strategy:** The pattern of decisions that defines your objectives as a sales organization. Strategy clarifies your pathways to growth and begins with a clear understanding of customer demands, potential and targeting. To execute your strategies, however, you'll have to ensure the right measures and performance management systems are in place.

- **Structure:** A determination of roles, resources and territories in relation to targeted markets and objectives. Market coverage requirements drive structure.

- **Talent:** A commitment to attract, develop and retain the right people in a highly competitive market for skilled sales professionals.

- **Motivation:** Clarifying the right rewards and compensation, when needs, interests and aspirations differ — sometimes, tremendously — by individual.

- **Enablement:** Putting in place the messaging skills, process and professional support, and tools and technologies necessary to perform effectively.

Smart design ensures your sales organization is fully armed to win. You'll address the issues of mindset, skillset and toolset — issues that collectively contribute to an organization's culture of performance. While sustained success also requires bold leadership, these design factors are the levers sales leaders such as you must pull to achieve your objectives.

That's not all. You're also challenged to rethink how you engage prospective buyers and how virtual selling practices enable you to support them more effectively on their journey. You are challenged to make the "Empathic Shift": getting deep into the buyer's world. As guide and adviser, you are challenged to address the key questions that emerge at every stage of a decision cycle.

That's not easy to do when one is always looking from the inside—out instead of the outside—in. It's vital, therefore, to clarify the costs and consequences of standing still. Why? Because inertial forces are always your greatest enemy. Indeed, 60% of deals end in no decision, according to research firm SBI.[18]

Buyer indecision is a challenge you must overcome, but you can't do that if you are overloading your prospect with tales of a fabulous future as opposed to clarifying the implications of today's unpleasant present. As a provocateur, you have to get deep into your buyer's world to determine if the present state is unsafe and unsustainable. If you can demonstrate it is, then you can create a sense of urgency. You will then have conquered your greatest enemy: inertia.

The game is afoot, as Sherlock Holmes would say. Sales leaders and sales strategists now have an opportunity to transform companies and shake up business in a powerful way. We've heard a lot about disruptive innovation in recent years. Disruption is now entering the world of sales and revenue production more broadly.

Money is on the move. Companies must now go upstream to grow strategic accounts and downstream to achieve greater market coverage. The portfolio of investments in sales operations and revenue production is being rebalanced.

The question for you is this: Are you making the investments necessary to propel your company forward in this era of perpetual disruption? Hopefully, this briefing book provided some useful guidance as you consider how to rebalance your own sales investment portfolio.

Acknowledgements

We interviewed or were influenced by a number of industry pioneers and transformational sales leaders. We've sought the counsel of CEOs, CSOs, CMOs, CROs and COOs. And we've drawn on the incisive perspectives of strategists, analysts and authors. They all helped shape and refine our thinking.

We are grateful to: Shimon Abouzaglo, Ardath Albee, Jon Allen, Phillip Andersen, Scott Armour, Lauren Bailey, Ralph Barsi, Massoud Bavar, Chris Beall, Matt Benelli, Trish Bertuzzi, Julie Brewer, Dan Burrill, Joanne Black, Chris Boudreaux, Zach Bowling, Richard Brasser, Judy Buchholz, Joe Bush, BJ Bushur, Bruce Church, Todd Cione, Bruce Cleveland, Elay Cohen, Linda Connly, Bill Crawford, Megan Dahlen, Donal Daly, Claire Daniaux, Tom Dekle, Doug Devitre, Matt Dixon, Dr. Howard Dover, Jennifer Dubow, Dean Dzurilla, Craig Elias, Dave Elkington, Cindy Fahrner, Josiane Feigon, John Ferrara, Colleen Francis, Dan Freund, Jeff Freund, Paul Friga, Kevin Gaither, Joe Galvin, Barb Giamanco, Paul Greenberg, Dustin Grosse, Gerhard Gschwandtner, Peter Guy, Lori Harmon, Alice Heiman, Matt Heinz, Karen Henken, Carlos Hidalgo, Brent Holloway, Jack Keen, Keenan, Kraig Kleeman, Jill Konrath, Hilarie Koplow-McAdams, Ken Krogue, Sid Kumar, Anthony Leaper, Avery Learner, Lars Leckie, Ron Lee, Ian Levine, Sharon Little, Matt Lockhart, Michael Lodato, Paul Macura, Darlene Mann, Josie Marshburn, Tino Mathew, Dan McDade, Shelley McNary, Pam McPherson, Adam Metz, Jon Miller, Kelly Molander, Lane Monson, Geoffrey Moore, Preston Moore, Martin Moran, Jacob Morgan, Sharon Drew Morgen, Sudipta Mukherjee, Irene Murphy, Ben Nachbaur, Shawn Naggiar, Nancy Nardin, Adam Needles, Laura Nuhaan, Liz Gelb O'Connor, Michael Ojile, Bubba Page, Tony Pante, Don Peppers, Bob Perkins, Erik Peterson, Dr. Rob Peterson, Dr. Natalie Petouhoff, Cliff Pollan, Denis Pombriant, Robert Racine, Larry Reeves, Jake Reni, Barry Rhein, Steve Richard, Lori Richardson, Tim Riesterer, Gordon Ritter, Mark Roberge, Justin Roff-Marsh, Craig Rosenberg, Aaron Ross, Thomas Rousseau, Jill Rowley, Avanish Sahai, Giovanna Sangiorgi, Kathleen Schaub, Erica Ruliffson Schultz, David Meerman Scott, Natasha Sekkat, Howard Sewell, Koka Sexton, Jamie Shanks, Tibor Shanto, Kurt Shaver, Clara Shih, Justin Shriber, MJ Shutte, David Skok, Michael Skok, Gary Smyth, Amy Spychalla, Colleen Stanley, Ingrid Steinbergs, David Sterenfeld, Leslie Talbot, Jeff Thull, Barry Trailer, Jeff Travis, Thierry van Herwijnen, Brian Vellmure, Ralf VonSosen, Julio Viskovich, Lesley Young, Daniel Zamudio and Teddy Zmrhal.

We are especially indebted to Charissa Franklin, Lee Sellers and our teams, who work alongside us every day to make Next Era Selling a reality for our clients. We also want to thank our book-production team — Marcia Egan, Jaime Hammond, Lauren Hauptman and Russell Moore — for keeping us on track and ensuring the editing and designs were on target. Finally, we would be remiss if we didn't thank our spouses. It is not the easiest thing to be married to someone who is often unavailable on evenings and weekends, because they are working on a book.

Endnotes

1. Michael Hammer, *The Agenda: What Every Business Must Do to Dominate the Decade* (Crown Business, 2002).

2. Debbie Qaqish, *Rise of the Revenue Marketer* (BookLogix, 2013).

3. Marisa Kopec and Jennifer Rose, *SiriusDecisions' 2015 B-to-B Buying Study,* SiriusDecisions, 2015.

4. R. Buckminster Fuller, *Synergetics: Explorations in the Geometry of Thinking* (Macmillan, 1975).

5. Steve W. Martin, "The Trend that is Changing Sales," *Harvard Business Review,* November 4, 2013.

6. David Skok, "How Sales Complexity Impacts Your Startup's Viability," *For Entrepreneurs* blog, 2010.

7. Chad Albrecht, Anneke Seley, Kyle Heller, *Outside In: The Rise of the Inside Sales Team,* Reality Works Group and ZS Associates, 2014.

8. Elay Cohen, *Saleshood: How Winning Managers Inspire Sales Teams to Succeed* (Greenleaf Book Group Press, 2014).

9. Barry Trailer, *2016 Sales Performance Optimization Study,* CSO Insights/MHI Global. 2016.

10. Craig Rosenberg, *The Sales Development Team: A Proven Framework for Success,* TOPO and SalesLoft, 2015.

11. James W. Phillips, David Elkington, Ken Krogue, *2014 Lead Response Report,* InsideSales.com, 2014.

12. Bob Perkins, *2013 Inside Sales Top Challenges: A Survey of Leaders and Representatives,* American Association of Inside Sales Professionals, 2013.

13. Joseph Rago, "Status Reporter: An Interview with Tom Wolfe," *Wall Street Journal,* March 11, 2016.

14. Eugene Kim, "Salesforce CEO Marc Benioff Says His Company is Outselling Oracle Because of this Huge Change in Sales," *Business Insider,* February 26, 2106.

15. Scott Santucci, Bradford Holmes, Daniel Feldman, *Executive Buyer Insight Study: Are Salespeople Prepared for Executive Conversations?,* Forrester Research, 2012.

16. John Care and Aron Bohlig, *Mastering Technical Sales* (Artech House Publishers, 2008).

17. Matthew Dixon and Berent Adamson, The Challenger Sale: Taking control of the Customer Conversation (Portfolio, 2011).

18. Amanda Wilson, "The New Rules of Sales Execution: Stop Enabling and Start Executing," *Sales and Marketing Management,* January 20, 2014.

About the Authors

Anneke Seley is CEO and founder of Reality Works Group (www.realityworksgroup.com), a next-generation sales consultancy, and coauthor of *Sales 2.0: Improve Business Results Using Innovative Sales Practices and Technology* (Wiley 2008). She was Oracle's 12th employee and designer of the company's pioneering inside selling organization, which serves as a model for many of today's fastest growing companies.

Britton Manasco is CEO and founder of Visible Impact (www.visibleimpact.com), a strategic marketing and sales enablement firm focused on making sales conversations matter. Prior to launching Visible Impact, Britton held thought-leadership roles with Corporate Visions (specialists in strategic messaging), Prime Resource Group (specialists in the complex sale), and Peppers and Rogers Group (specialists in customer strategy).

CPSIA information can be obtained
at www.ICGtesting.com
Printed in the USA
LVOW05*0455191017
552651LV00005BC/6/P